Zeitschrift für Betriebswirtschaft

Special Issue 5/2009

Entrepreneurial Finance

ZfB-Special Issues

6/2006 Rechnungslegung nach internationalen Grundsätzen
Herausgeber: Norbert Krawitz
180 Seiten. ISBN 3 8349 0425 6

1/2007 Der Ehrbare Kaufmann: Modernes Leitbild für Unternehmer?
Herausgeber: Joachim Schwalbach/Günter Fandel
140 Seiten. ISBN 3 8349 0659 X

2/2007 Innovation, Orientation, Innovativeness and Innovation Success
Herausgeber: Holger Ernst/Hans Georg Gemünden
156 Seiten. ISBN 3 8349 0698 0

3/2007 Direct Marketing
Herausgeber: Manfred Krafft/Jürgen Gerdes
192 Seiten. ISBN 3 8349 0728 6

4/2007 Open Innovation between and within Organizations
Herausgeber: Holger Ernst/Hans Georg Gemünden
140 Seiten. ISBN 3 8349 0731 6

5/2007 Hochschulrechnung und Hochschulcontrolling
Herausgeber: Hans-Ulrich Küpper
188 Seiten. ISBN 3 8349 0778 2

6/2007 Empirische Studien zum Management in mittelständischen Unternehmen
Herausgeber: Horst Albach/Peter Letmathe
140 Seiten. ISBN 3 8349 0799 5

1/2008 Economics and Management of Education
Herausgeber: Dominique Demougin/Oliver Fabel
192 Seiten. ISBN 3 8349 0904 1

2/2008 Corporate Governance in der Praxis mittelständischer Unternehmen
Herausgeber: Horst Albach/Peter Letmathe
136 Seiten. ISBN 3 8349 0931 2

3/2008 Corporate Social Responsibility
Herausgeber: Joachim Schwalbach
112 Seiten. ISBN 3 8349 1044 9

4/2008 Forschungsperspektiven der betriebswirtschaftlichen Logistik
Herausgeber: Hartmut Stadtler/Herbert Kotzab
164 Seiten. ISBN 3 8349 1157 7

5/2008 Erich Gutenbergs Theorie der Unternehmung – Wirkungen auf die heutige Betriebswirtschaftslehre –
Herausgeber: Joachim Reese/Marion Steven
112 Seiten. ISBN 3 8349 1187 9

6/2008 50 Years after MM: Recent Developments in Corporate Finance
Herausgeber: Wolfgang Breuer/Marc Gürtler
188 Seiten. ISBN 3 8349 1426 2

1/2009 International Entrepreneurship
Herausgeber: Andreas Al-Laham/Martin K. Welge/Joachim Schwalbach
196 Seiten. ISBN 3 8349 1474 6

2/2009 Management von Familienunternehmen
Herausgeber: Peter Witt
168 Seiten. ISBN 3 8349 1620 X

3/2009 Operations Research in der Betriebswirtschaft – Neue Anwendungsgebiete und Ergebnisse
Herausgeber: Heinrich Kuhn/Hartmut Stadtler/Gerhard Wäscher
144 Seiten. ISBN 3 8349 1723 0

4/2009 Rational Inefficiencies
Herausgeber: Günter Fandel
136 Seiten. ISBN 3 8349 1856 3

Entrepreneurial Finance

Herausgeber
Prof. Dr. Wolfgang Breuer
Prof. Dr. Malte Brettel

Die Deutsche Bibliothek – CIP-Einheitsaufnahme

Zeitschrift für Betriebswirtschaft : ZfB. – Wiesbaden :
Gabler/GWV Fachverlage GmbH
Erscheint monatl. – Aufnahme nach Jg. 67, H. 3 (1997)
Reihe Ergänzungsheft: Zeitschrift für Betriebswirtschaft /
Ergänzungsheft. Fortlaufende Beil.: Betriebswirtschaftliches
Repetitorium. – Danach bis 1979: ZfB-Repetitorium
ISSN 0044-2372
2009, Special Issue 5. Entrepreneurial Finance
Herausgeber: Wolfgang Breuer, Malte Brettel – Wiesbaden: Gabler, 2009
(Zeitschrift für Betriebswirtschaft; 2009, Special Issue 5)

ISBN 978-3-8349-2005-8

Alle Rechte vorbehalten

© Gabler/GWV Fachverlage GmbH, Wiesbaden 2010
Lektorat: Susanne Kramer/Annelie Meisenheimer

Gabler ist Teil der Fachverlagsgruppe Springer Science+Business Media.

Das Werk einschließlich aller seiner Teile ist urheberrechtlich geschützt. Jede Verwertung außerhalb der engen Grenzen des Urheberrechtsgesetzes ist ohne Zustimmung des Verlags unzulässig und strafbar. Das gilt insbesondere für Vervielfältigungen, Übersetzungen, Mikroverfilmungen und die Einspeicherung und Verarbeitung in elektronischen Systemen.

http://www.gabler.de
http://www.zfb-online.de

Höchste inhaltliche und technische Qualität unserer Produkte ist unser Ziel. Bei der Produktion und Verbreitung unserer Bücher wollen wir die Umwelt schonen: Dieses Buch ist auf säurefreiem und chlorfrei gebleichtem Papier gedruckt. Die Einschweißfolie besteht aus Polyäthylen und damit aus organischen Grundstoffen, die weder bei der Herstellung noch bei der Verbrennung Schadstoffe freisetzen.

Die Wiedergabe von Gebrauchsnamen, Handelsnamen, Warenbezeichnungen usw. in diesem Werk berechtigt auch ohne besondere Kennzeichnung nicht zu der Annahme, dass solche Namen im Sinne der Warenzeichen- und Markenschutz-Gesetzgebung als frei zu betrachten wären und daher von jedermann benutzt werden dürften.

ISBN 978-3-8349-2005-8

INHALTSVERZEICHNIS

VII Editorial

1 **Venture Capital Financing and Capital Structure Choice: A Panel Study of German Growth Companies**
Prof. Dr. Dietmar Grichnik, Vallendar, Prof. Dr. Dirk Schiereck, Darmstadt, and Dr. Andreas Wenzel, Witten/Herdecke

25 **Linking Incorporated Cultural and Financial Capital of the Entrepreneur in a New Venture Creation Context: A Cross-Country Comparison**
Dipl.-Kff. Mag. Malgorzata A. Wdowiak, Univ.-Prof. Dr. Erich J. Schwarz, Dr. Robert J. Breitenecker, Klagenfurt, Austria, and PD Dr. Rainer Harms, Enschede, The Netherlands

53 **Angels or Demons? Evidence on the Impact of Private Equity Firms on Employment**
Dr. Eva Lutz and Prof. Dr. Dr. Ann-Kristin Achleitner, München

83 **Antecedents of Style Drift in Private Equity Investments**
Dr. Rainer Lauterbach, Frankfurt am Main, Prof. Dr. Isabell M. Welpe, Munich, and Dipl.-Kfm. Benjamin Langer, Frankfurt am Main

101 **Financing Young Biotechnology Companies: Public Support and Venture Capital in Comparison**
Dr. Oliver Heneric, Weinheim, and Prof. Dr. Peter Witt, Dortmund

XI GRUNDSÄTZE UND ZIELE
XIII HERAUSGEBER/EDITORIAL BOARD
XIV IMPRESSUM/HINWEISE FÜR AUTOREN

Unternehmensbesteuerung kompakt und fundiert

WWW.GABLER.D

Kraft, Cornelia / Kraft, Gerhard
Grundlagen der Unternehmensbesteuerung
Die wichtigsten Steuerarten und ihr Zusammenwirken
3., vollst. überarb. Aufl. 2009. XXVIII, 376 S.
Mit 164 Abb. u. 32 Tab. Br.
EUR 28,90
ISBN 978-3-8349-0597-0

Die Autoren stellen alle relevanten Steuerarten dar, auf denen die deutsche Unternehmensbesteuerung basiert. Darüber hinaus wird das Zusammenwirken der einzelnen Steuerarten in Bezug auf die Gesamtsteuerbelastung von Unternehmen herausgearbeitet. Zahlreiche Übersichten, Schaubilder und Beispiele verdeutlichen Strukturen und Zusammenhänge. Die kompakte Wissensvermittlung führt schnell zu fundierten Kenntnissen der wichtigsten deutschen Steuerarten. Die dritte Auflage befindet sich auf dem Rechtsstand 01.01.2009 und berücksichtigt alle relevanten steuerlichen Regelungen und Gesetzesentwürfe. Insbesondere auf das Unternehmensteuerreformgesetz 2008 und die Erbschaftsteuerreform 2009 gehen die Autoren ausführlich ein.

Der Inhalt
- Das deutsche Steuersystem
- Einkommensteuer
- Körperschaftsteuer
- Gewerbesteuer
- Besteuerung des Unternehmensertrags
- Erbschaft- und Schenkungsteuer
- Grundsteuer
- Umsatzsteuer
- Grunderwerbsteuer

Die Autoren
Prof. Dr. Cornelia Kraft lehrt Betriebliche Steuerlehre und Unternehmensprüfung an der FH Bielefeld. Sie ist außerdem selbstständige Steuerberaterin.
Prof. Dr. Gerhard Kraft lehrt ABWL und Betriebswirtschaftliche Steuerlehre an der Martin-Luther-Universität Halle-Wittenberg. Darüber hinaus ist er Steuerberater und Wirtschaftsprüfer.

Einfach bestellen:
kerstin.kuchta@gwv-fachverlage.de
Telefon +49(0)611. 7878-626

KOMPETENZ IN SACHEN WIRTSCHAFT

Editorial

While formerly somewhat neglected, for the last few years, researchers in business administration have increasingly become aware of the central role of small and medium enterprises for the prosperity of an economy. As a consequence, "entrepeneurship" has grown a most relevant sub-discipline in business administration. In this special issue of the Zeitschrift für Betriebswirtschaft, we want to focus on the specific problems in the field of finance that are essential for small and medium enterprises. To be more precise, this issue consists of five articles that focus on different problems in the field of entrepreneurial finance.

The first two articles address the issue of how to finance small and medium enterprises. From a theoretical viewpoint, there are good reasons why the capital structure decision of growth companies should be different from that of mature companies. The aim of the article **"Venture Capital Financing and Capital Structure Choice: A Panel Study of German Growth Companies"** by *Dietmar Grichnik, Dirk Schiereck*, and *Andreas Wenzel* is to offer an empirical examination of this issue. In particular, they analyze 1) how the debt ratio of growth companies is influenced by a comprehensive set of capital structure determinants and 2) if capital structure determinants differ between venture capital (VC) financed and non-VC-financed companies. In order to do so, the authors use a unique sample of 155 German growth companies during the time before their initial public offering (IPO) and employ fixed and random effects panel regression methods. *Grichnik et al.* provide evidence that ownership structure among venture capitalists and insiders, e.g. entrepreneurs and/or managers, significantly impacts the debt ratio of growth companies before the IPO, but not thereafter. Higher relative equity shares of VC investors are accompanied by lower debt ratios. While higher tangibility is associated with higher debt ratios, higher liquidity, profitability, and risk imply lower levels of debt. Moreover, it appears that the relationships between the capital structure and company age, size and growth are different between companies financed with VC and those without.

In their article **"Linking Incorporated Cultural and Financial Capital of the Entrepreneur in a New Venture Creation Context: A Cross-Country Comparison"**, *Malgorzata A. Wdowiak, Erich J. Schwarz, Robert J. Breitenecker*, and *Rainer Harms* address the issue of how a founder's decision of initial financial capital for a new venture is influenced by his or her cultural background. According to the theory of cultural capital, cultural habits (expressed by values), knowledge and skills developed in the process of cultural socialization, and work experience are crucial to behavior and outcomes in the context of social actions performed by the individual. Based on that theory, the authors explore the effects of individualistic and collectivistic values, knowledge acquired through work experience, and entrepreneurial skills on the amount of initial financial capital. They test their hypotheses in two countries with different cultural environments and at different stages of economic development: in Austria (n = 127), which has a longer individualistic tradition, and in Poland (n = 136) with its communist, collectivistic legacy. The empirical findings imply that collectivistic values, entrepreneurial skills, and industry experience have a significant impact on the amount of initial financial capital in both countries. In the comparative country context, especially the relationship between industry experience of Austrian founders and the amount of initial financial capital proved to be stronger than that of their Polish counterparts. In sum, by this study the authors are able to close an important research gap, as the issue of a founder's culturally bounded behavior has not been examined to a satisfying degree up to now.

The next two articles take up the decision situation of private equity firms as central investors for small and medium enterprises. In 2005, statements by *Franz Müntefering*, a leading Social Democrat, opened up a harsh public discussion about private equity in Germany which became known as the locust debate. This debate quickly spread to the U.K. and other European countries and evolved around the accusation that private equity firms achieve exceptional rates of returns through brutal cost reductions and at the expense of employees. In their article, **"Angels or Demons? Evidence on the Impact of Private Equity Firms on Employment"**, *Eva Lutz* and *Ann-Kristin Achleitner* take a closer look at this issue by surveying 49 studies that focus on the potential employment effects of private equity financing. These studies are focused on different aspects of employment and are based on a variety of methodologies as well as samples representing e.g. different types of buyouts and geographies. The analysis of similarities and differences of the studies reveals manifold consequences of private equity on employment with the impact varying across different employment indicators and between geographies. Summarizing, it is not possible to label private equity firms either positively or negatively – as "angels" or "demons" – as this would not take account of their complex and heterogeneous effects on employees post-buyout.

Similar to investment funds in other asset classes, private equity funds (PEF) usually have an investment focus or "investment style". The focus can be on anything between specific industries, geographic regions, or a particular development stage of target companies. Investors are interested in the focus of a PEF so that they can control the risk-return profile of their total investments. Drifts of PEF from the original investment focus are therefore something which is generally contrary to the interests of investors. In their article, **"Antecedents of Style Drift in Private Equity Investments"**, *Rainer Lauterbach*, *Isabell Welpe*, and *Benjamin Langer* address the question as to why PEF at times drift from their original focus nonetheless. Employing a dataset of 426 investments in the time span between 1983 and 2003, they find evidence for three antecedents to style drifts: investment fund size (positive), investment fund experience (negative) and amount invested in the target company (positive). Given that style drifts are a regular occurrence in the private equity industry, the results of this research holds important practical implications.

Because of their high economic relevance, small and medium enterprises are in the focus of public support measures. This topic is addressed by the last article of this issue. Biotechnology is a promising industry with high growth potential. Accordingly, both governments and investors are highly interested in moving this sector forward. Given the high risk and the extensive capital requirements associated with biotechnology ventures, usually venture capital is the most commonly used financing form. However, considering the significant public benefit that is induced by successful biotechnology ventures, governments have developed financial schemes to foster the development of this industry. A frequently voiced justification for this involvement is that government can prevent market failure in cases where there are ventures with promising prospects for the public good, but where risk is too high for regular venture capital funds. In their article, **"Financing Young Biotechnology Companies: Public Support and Venture Capital in Comparison"**, *Oliver Heneric* and *Peter Witt* investigate whether or not this contention is correct. Using a self-generated database of 1,529 German biotechnology companies and employing probit regressions, they find that in fact the investment criteria of public institutions are not different from those of regular venture capital funds. In a nutshell, this implies that present German government involvement effectively does not serve to reduce market failure in the financing of promising but risky biotechnology ventures. Instead, it rather provides support to companies who already have access to venture capital.

Summarizing, the articles of this special issue offer an excellent overview of research questions lying at the very heart of entrepreneurial finance and thus may serve as the starting point for further interesting investigations.

Wolfgang Breuer
Malte Brettel

Alle wichtigen Methoden der Marketing-Forschung auf einen Blick ↗

WWW.GABLER.DE

Raab, Gerhard / Unger, Alexander / Unger, Fritz
Methoden der Marketing-Forschung
Grundlagen und Praxisbeispiele
2., überarb. Aufl. 2009. X, 477 S. Mit 184 Abb.
Br. EUR 39,90
ISBN 978-3-8349-0992-3

Gerhard Raab, Alexander und Fritz Unger geben einen umfassenden Einblick in die relevanten Methoden der Marketing-Forschung. Im Mittelpunkt stehen Fragen der allgemeinen Methodenlehre, der Datenanalyse auf Basis moderner Auswertungsprogramme sowie Anwendungsbeispiele praktischer Marketing-Forschung. Die Autoren gehen auch auf Aspekte internationaler Marketing-Forschung ein. Die statistischen Analyse-Methoden nehmen breiten Raum ein, dennoch sind alle Kapitel ohne umfassende Vorkenntnisse verständlich. In die zweite Auflage wurde der aktuelle Wissensstand aus Forschung und Praxis eingearbeitet.

Der Inhalt
- Allgemeine Methodenlehre
- Auswahltechniken und Datenerfassung
- Methoden der Datenanalyse
- Methoden kulturvergleichender Forschung
- Anwendungsbeispiele im Marketing

Die Autoren
Prof. Dr. Gerhard Raab lehrt an der Fachhochschule Ludwigshafen Marketing und Marktpsychologie, insbes. am Studiengang „Betriebswirtschaft im Praxisverbund" (BiP).
Dr. Alexander Unger lehrt an der Fachhochschule Ludwigshafen Statistik und Psychologie.
Prof. Dr. Fritz Unger lehrt Betriebswirtschaftslehre und Marketing im Studiengang Berufsintegrierendes Studium (BIS) Betriebswirtschaft an der Fachhochschule Ludwigshafen.

Einfach bestellen:
kerstin.kuchta@gwv-fachverlage.de
Telefon +49(0)611. 7878-626

KOMPETENZ IN SACHEN WIRTSCHAFT   GABLER

GRUNDSÄTZE UND ZIELE

Die **Zeitschrift für Betriebswirtschaft (ZfB)** ist eine der ältesten deutschen Fachzeitschriften der Betriebswirtschaftslehre. Sie wurde im Jahre 1924 von Fritz Schmidt begründet und von Wilhelm Kalveram, Erich Gutenberg und Horst Albach fortgeführt. Sie wird heute von 14 Universitätsprofessoren, die als **Department Editors** fungieren, herausgegeben. Dem **Editorial Board** gehören namhafte Persönlichkeiten aus Universität und Wirtschaftspraxis an. Die Fachvertreter stammen aus den USA, Japan und Europa.

Die ZfB verfolgt das Ziel, die **Forschung auf dem Gebiet der Betriebswirtschaftslehre** anzuregen sowie zur Verbreitung und Anwendung ihrer Ergebnisse beizutragen. Sie betont die Einheit des Faches; enger und einseitiger Spezialisierung in der Betriebswirtschaftslehre will sie entgegenwirken. Die Zeitschrift dient dem **Gedankenaustausch zwischen Wissenschaft und Unternehmenspraxis**. Sie will die betriebswirtschaftliche Forschung auf wichtige betriebswirtschaftliche Probleme in der Praxis aufmerksam machen und sie durch Anregungen aus der Unternehmenspraxis befruchten.

In der ZfB können auch englischsprachige Aufsätze veröffentlicht werden. Die Herausgeber begrüßen die Einreichung englischsprachiger Beiträge von deutschen und internationalen Wissenschaftlern. Durch die Zusammenfassungen in englischer Sprache sind die deutschsprachigen Aufsätze der ZfB auch internationalen Referatenorganen zugänglich. Im Journal of Economic Literature werden die Aufsätze der ZfB zum Beispiel laufend referiert.

Die Qualität der Aufsätze in der ZfB wird durch die Herausgeber und einen Kreis renommierter Gutachter gewährleistet. Das **Begutachtungsverfahren** ist doppelt verdeckt und wahrt damit die Anonymität von Autoren wie Gutachtern gemäß den international üblichen Standards. Jeder Beitrag wird von zwei Fachgutachtern beurteilt. Bei abweichenden Gutachten wird ein Drittgutachter bestellt. Die Department Editors entscheiden auf der Grundlage der Gutachten eigenverantwortlich über die Annahme und Ablehnung der von ihnen betreuten Manuskripte. Sie können Beiträge auch ohne Begutachtungsverfahren ablehnen, wenn diese formal oder inhaltlich von den Vorgaben der ZfB abweichen.

Die ZfB veröffentlicht im Einklang mit diesen Grundsätzen und Zielen:
- **Aufsätze** zu theoretischen und praktischen Fragen der Betriebswirtschaftslehre einschließlich von Arbeiten junger Wissenschaftler, denen sie ein Forum für die Diskussion und die Verbreitung ihrer Forschungsergebnisse eröffnet,
- **Ergebnisse der Diskussion** aktueller betriebswirtschaftlicher Themen zwischen Wissenschaftlern und Praktikern,
- **Berichte** über den Einsatz wissenschaftlicher Instrumente und Konzepte bei der Lösung von betriebswirtschaftlichen Problemen in der Praxis,
- **Schilderungen von Problemen** aus der Praxis zur Anregung der betriebswirtschaftlichen Forschung,
- **„State of the Art"-Artikel,** in denen Entwicklung und Stand der Betriebswirtschaftslehre eines Teilgebietes dargelegt werden.

Die ZfB informiert ihre Leser über **Neuerscheinungen** in der Betriebswirtschafslehre und der Management Literatur durch ausführliche Rezensionen und Kurzbesprechungen und berichtet in ihrem **Nachrichtenteil** regelmäßig über betriebswirtschaftliche Tagungen, Seminare und Konferenzen sowie über persönliche Veränderungen vorwiegend an den Hochschulen. Darüber hinaus werden auch Nachrichten für Studenten und Wirtschaftspraktiker veröffentlicht, die Bezug zur Hochschule haben.

HERAUSGEBER/EDITORIAL BOARD

Editor-in-Chief

Prof. Dr. Dr. h.c. Günter Fandel ist Universitätsprofessor und Inhaber des Lehrstuhls für Betriebswirtschaft, insbesondere Produktions- und Investitionstheorie an der FernUniversität in Hagen. Seine Hauptarbeitsgebiete sind Industriebetriebslehre, Produktionsmanagement und Hochschulmanagement.

Department Editors

Prof. Dr. Wolfgang Breuer ist Universitätsprofessor und Inhaber des Lehrstuhls für Betriebswirtschaftslehre, insb. Betriebliche Finanzwirtschaft, an der Rheinisch-Westfälischen Technischen Hochschule Aachen. Seine Hauptarbeitsgebiete sind Finanzierungs- und Investitionstheorie sowie Portfolio- und Risikomanagement.

Prof. Dr. Holger Ernst ist Inhaber des Lehrstuhls für Betriebswirtschaftslehre, insbesondere Technologie- und Innovationsmanagement an der Wissenschaftlichen Hochschule für Unternehmensführung – Otto-Beisheim-Hochschule – (WHU) in Vallendar.

Prof. Dr. Oliver Fabel ist Universitätsprofessor und Inhaber des Lehrstuhls für Personalwirtschaft mit Internationaler Schwerpunktsetzung am Institut für Betriebswirtschaftslehre der Universität Wien. Seine Hauptarbeitsgebiete sind Personal-, Organisations- und Bildungsökonomik.

Prof. Dr. Dr. h.c. Günter Fandel, s.o.

Prof. Dr. Armin Heinzl ist Universitätsprofessor und Inhaber des Lehrstuhls für Allgemeine Betriebswirtschaftslehre und Wirtschaftsinformatik an der Universität Mannheim. Seine Hauptarbeitsgebiete sind Wirtschaftsinformatik, Organisationslehre sowie Logistik.

Prof. Dr. Harald Hruschka ist Universitätsprofessor und Inhaber des Lehrstuhls für Betriebswirtschaftslehre mit dem Schwerpunkt Marketing an der Universität Regensburg. Sein Hauptarbeitsgebiet bezieht sich auf Marktreaktionsmodelle unter Einschluss semiparametrischer und hierarchischer Bayes'scher Ansätze.

Prof. Dr. Norbert Krawitz ist Universitätsprofessor und Inhaber des Lehrstuhls für Betriebswirtschaftslehre mit dem Schwerpunkt Betriebswirtschaftliche Steuerlehre und Prüfungswesen an der Universität Siegen. Seine Hauptarbeitsgebiete sind Rechnungslegung, Wirtschaftsprüfung und betriebswirtschaftliche Steuerlehre.

Prof. Dr. Dr. h.c. Hans-Ulrich Küpper ist Universitätsprofessor und Direktor des Instituts für Produktionswirtschaft und Controlling der Universität München. Seine Hauptarbeitsgebiete sind Unternehmensrechnung, Controlling und Hochschulmanagement.

Prof. Dr. Werner Pascha ist Universitätsprofessor und Inhaber des Lehrstuhls für Ostasienwirtschaft / Wirtschaftspolitik an der Universität Duisburg-Essen.

Prof. Dr. Joachim Schwalbach ist Universitätsprofessor und Inhaber des Lehrstuhls für Internationales Management an der Humboldt-Universität zu Berlin.

Prof. Dr. Hartmut Stadtler ist Universitätsprofessor und Inhaber des Instituts für Logistik und Transport an der Universität Hamburg. Seine Hauptarbeitsgebiete sind die Logistik, die Unternehmensplanung und die unternehmensübergreifende Planung im Rahmen des Supply Chain Management sowie deren Unterstützung durch Softwaresysteme (z.B. Advanced Planning Systeme).

Prof. Dr. Stefan Winter ist Universitätsprofessor und Inhaber des Lehrstuhls für Human Resource Management an der Ruhr-Universität in Bochum. Seine Hauptarbeitsgebiete sind die Analyse von Anreizstrukturen in Unternehmen, Gestaltung von Vergütungssystemen für Führungskräfte sowie die Institutionenökonomische Analyse von Personal- und Organisationsproblemen.

Prof. Dr. Peter Witt ist Universitätsprofessor und Inhaber des Lehrstuhls für Innovations- und Gründungsmanagement an der Universität Dortmund. Seine Hauptarbeitsgebiete sind Entrepreneurship, Gründungsfinanzierung und Familienunternehmen.

Prof. Dr. Uwe Zimmermann ist Hochschulprofessor und Leiter des Instituts für Mathematische Optimierung an der Technischen Universität Braunschweig. Seine Hauptarbeitsgebiete sind die Lineare, Kombinatorische und Diskrete Optimierung und ihre Anwendung auf komplexe Systeme in Verkehr und Logistik.

Editorial Board

Prof. (em.) Dr. Dr. h.c. mult. Horst Albach (Chairman)
Prof. Alain Burlaud
Prof. Dr. Dr. h.c. Santiago Garcia Echevarria
Prof. Dr. Lars Engwall
Dr. Dieter Heuskel
Dr. Detlef Hunsdiek
Prof. Dr. Don Jacobs
Prof. Dr. Eero Kasanen
Dr. Bernd-Albrecht v. Maltzan
Prof. Dr. Koji Okubayashi
Hans Botho von Portatius
Prof. Dr. Oleg D. Prozenko
Prof. (em.) Dr. Hermann Sabel
Prof. Dr. Adolf Stepan
Dr. med. Martin Zügel

IMPRESSUM/HINWEISE FÜR AUTOREN

Verlag

Gabler/GWV Fachverlage GmbH,
Abraham-Lincoln-Straße 46, 65189 Wiesbaden,
http://www.gabler.de
http://www.zfb-online.de
Geschäftsführer: Dr. Ralf Birkelbach, Albrecht F. Schirmacher
Verlagsbereichsleitung Buch, Journals, Seminare, Online:
Maria Akhavan-Hezavei
Gesamtleitung Produktion: Christian Staral
Gesamtleitung Vertrieb: Gabriel Göttlinger

Editor-in-Chief:
Professor Dr. Dr. h.c. Günter Fandel
FernUniversität in Hagen
Fakultät für Wirtschaftswissenschaft
58084 Hagen
Tel: 02331/987-2625, Fax: 02331/987-2375
E-Mail: ZfB@FernUni-Hagen.de

Administration Manuscript Central™
Sebastian Bartussek, Tel.: 02331/987-2652,
Fax: 02331/987-2575, E-Mail: Sebastian.Bartussek@FernUni-Hagen.de

Redaktion: Annelie Meisenheimer, Tel.: 0611/7878-232,
Fax: 0611/7878-411, E-Mail: Annelie.Meisenheimer@gabler.de

Abonnentenbetreuung: Stefanie Druffelsmeyer, Tel.: 05241/801968,
Fax: 05241/809620

Produktmanagement: Melanie Engelhard-Gökalp,
Tel.: 0611/7878-315, Fax: 0611/7878-440,
E-Mail: melanie.engelhard-goekalp@gabler.de

Anzeigenleitung: Stefan Strussione, Tel.: 0611/7878-157,
Fax: 0611/7878-430, E-Mail: Stefan.Strussione@gwv-fachverlage.de

Anzeigendisposition: Monika Dannenberger,
Tel.: 0611/7878-148, Fax: 0611/7878-430,
E-Mail: Monika.Dannenberger@gwv-fachverlage.de

Es gilt die Anzeigenpreisliste vom 1. 1. 2006.

Produktion/Layout: Sandra Kraut

Bezugsmöglichkeiten: Die Zeitschrift erscheint monatlich. Das Abonnement kann jederzeit zur nächsten erreichbaren Ausgabe schriftlich mit Nennung der Kundennummer gekündigt werden. Eine schriftliche Bestätigung erfolgt nicht. Zuviel gezahlte Beträge für nicht gelieferte Ausgaben werden zurückerstattet. Jährlich können 1 bis 6 Special Issues hinzukommen. Jedes Special Issue wird den Abonnenten mit einem Nachlass von 25% des jeweiligen Ladenpreises gegen Rechnung geliefert.

	Preise Inland:	Preise Ausland:
Einzelheft:	40,- Euro	46,- Euro
Studenten-*/Emeritus-Abo:	72,- Euro	92,- Euro
ausgewählte Verbände:**	176,- Euro	193,- Euro
Privat-Abo:	208,- Euro	235,- Euro
Lehrstuhl-Abo:	235,- Euro	261,- Euro
Bibliotheks-/Unternehmensabo:	407,- Euro	426,- Euro

* Studienbescheinigung
** auf Anfrage beim Verlag

© Gabler/GWV Fachverlage GmbH, Wiesbaden 2009.

Gabler ist Teil der Fachverlagsgruppe Springer Science+Business Media.

Alle Rechte vorbehalten. Kein Teil dieser Zeitschrift darf ohne schriftliche Genehmigung des Verlages vervielfältigt oder verbreitet werden. Unter dieses Verbot fällt insbesondere die gewerbliche Vervielfältigung per Kopie, die Aufnahme in elektronische Datenbanken und die Vervielfältigung auf CD-ROM und allen anderen elektronischen Datenträgern.

Satzherstellung: Fotosatz-Service Köhler GmbH,
97084 Würzburg.
Druck und Verarbeitung: Druckerei Krips, Meppel, Niederlande.

Gedruckt auf säurefreiem und chlorfrei gebleichtem Papier.

Printed in Europe

Hinweise für Autoren

1. Bitte beachten Sie die „Grundsätze und Ziele" der ZfB.

2. Einreichungen werden bei der ZfB ausschließlich über ein Online-Verfahren abgewickelt. Manuskripte – in deutscher oder englischer Sprache – können vom Autor unter http://mc.manuscriptcentral.com/zfb direkt in das Manuskriptverwaltungssystem hochgeladen werden. Hierbei ist insbesondere auf die Wahrung der Anonymität der zur Begutachtung eingereichten Vorlagen zu achten. Der Autor verpflichtet sich mit der Einsendung des Manuskripts unwiderruflich, das Manuskript bis zur Entscheidung über die Annahme nicht anderweitig zu veröffentlichen oder zur Veröffentlichung anzubieten. Diese Verpflichtung erlischt nicht durch Korrekturvorschläge im Begutachtungsverfahren.

3. Aufsätze, die im wesentlichen Ergebnisse von Dissertationen wiedergeben, werden nicht veröffentlicht. Um die Ergebnisse von Dissertationen breiter bekannt zu machen, hat die ZfB eine Rubrik „Dissertationen" im Besprechungsteil eingeführt. Hier werden vorzugsweise Erstgutachten von Dissertationen – in entsprechend gekürzter Form – abgedruckt.

4. Um die eingereichten Manuskripte in den Begutachtungsprozess geben bzw. diese im Manuskriptlauf zügig behandeln zu können, wird um Beachtung der folgenden Punkte gebeten: Gesamtlänge des Manuskriptes darf 25 DinA4 nicht überschreiten (bei ca. 3800 Zeichen pro Seite), Schriftart „Times New Roman", Schriftgröße 12, einfacher Zeilenabstand, jeweils 2,5 cm Außenrand, Angabe von Abbildungs- und Tabellenüberschriften (Abb. 1: Text; Tab. 1: Text etc.), eingebundene Objekte (insbes. Bild-, .ppt-, .xls-Dateien etc.) auch separat in Dateiform beifügen, das Hauptdokument muss in **anonymer** Form eingereicht werden, d.h. alle Autorennamen, Autoreninformationen und evtl. Danksagungen sind für die Begutachtung restlos zu streichen. Einhaltung der Gliederungssystematik: **1 Überschriftsebene 1** (12pt, fett, 2 Zeilen Abstand davor, 1 Zeile danach), *1.1 Überschriftsebene 2* (12pt, 1 Zeile Abstand davor, 1 Zeile danach), 1.1.1 Überschriftsebene 3 (12pt, kursiv, 1 Zeile Abstand davor, 1 Zeile danach), Spitzmarke: (12pt, fett mit Doppelpunkt zu Beginn des Absatzes, 1 Zeile Abstand davor). Harvard-Zitierweise, keine End- oder Fußnoten: Ein Autor: (vgl. Meier 2007) bzw. (Meier 2007, S. 30); Zwei Autoren: (vgl. Meier/Müller 2007) bzw. (Meier/Müller 2007, S. 30); Drei oder mehr Autoren: (vgl. Meier et al. 2007) bzw. (Meier et al. 2007, S. 30); Eventuelle Erläuterungen zu Textpassagen können weiterhin als Endnoten angehängt werden, sollten aber – soweit möglich – vermieden werden. Das Literaturverzeichnis muss in *Harvard Stil* bzw. *Basic Springer Reference Style* aufgebaut sein. Bei einer Wiedereinreichung eines Beitrags muss eine Stellungnahme zu den Gutachten beigelegt werden. Einreichung der Beitragsdatei als **Microsoft Word®-Datei** oder in einem Word®-kompatiblen Format; **kein (La)TeX. PDF-Dateien sind generell nicht geeignet und können auch nicht im Onlinesystem Manuscript Central™ hochgeladen werden.** Der Beitrag muss in folgender Reihenfolge aufgebaut sein: Erste Seite: prägnanter Beitragstitel in deutscher bzw. in englischer Sprache (max. 80 Zeichen; bei Bedarf: Angabe eines Untertitels), dem Beitrag vorgestellte einleitende „Zusammenfassung" bzw. einleitender „Abstract" (Fließtext, max. 15 Zeilen bzw. 1100 Zeichen), deutsche „Schlüsselwörter" (max. 5 Angaben) bzw. englische Keywords (max. 5 Angaben), JEL-Klassifikation (max. 3 Angaben); Ab Seite 2: Beitragstext, falls nötig: „Anmerkungen" als Endnoten (keine Fußnoten im Text), „Literaturverzeichnis", letzte Seite: (nur bei deutschsprachigen Beiträgen) enfällt bei englischsprachigen Beiträgen) prägnanter Beitragstitel in englischer Sprache (max. 80 Zeichen, bei Bedarf: Angabe eines Untertitels), „Abstract" in englischer Sprache (Fließtext, max. 15 Zeilen bzw. 1100 Zeichen). Zusätzlich sollten sowohl die Autorenfotos (in digitaler Form, 300dpi, mind. 640x480 Pixel) als auch die Autorenangaben (Titel, Name, Institut, Lehrstuhl, Adresse, Land, ggf. Arbeitsgebiete, Emailadresse und URL; insgesamt pro Autor max. 4 Zeilen) in separaten Dateien eingereicht werden. **Alle Kopf- und Fußzeilen sowie Seitenzahlen sind zu entfernen!**

5. Der Autor verpflichtet sich, die Korrekturfahnen innerhalb einer Woche zu lesen und die Mehrkosten für Korrekturen, die nicht vom Verlag zu vertreten sind, sowie die Kosten für die Korrektur durch einen Korrektor bei nicht terminrechter Rücksendung der Fahnenkorrektur zu übernehmen.

6. Der Autor ist damit einverstanden, dass sein Beitrag auch in der Zeitschrift auch durch Lizenzvergabe in anderen Zeitschriften (auch übersetzt), durch Nachdruck in Sammelbänden (z.B. zu Jubiläen der Zeitschrift oder des Verlages auch in Themenbänden), durch längere Auszüge in Büchern des Verlages auch zu Werbezwecken, durch Vervielfältigung und Verbreitung auf CD-ROM oder anderen Datenträgern, durch Speicherung auf Datennetzen, deren Weitergabe und dem Abruf von solchen Datenbanken während der Dauer des Urheberrechtsschutzes an dem Beitrag im In- und Ausland vom Verlag und seinen Lizenznehmern genutzt wird.

Venture Capital Financing and Capital Structure Choice: A Panel Study of German Growth Companies

Dietmar Grichnik, Dirk Schiereck, Andreas Wenzel

Abstract: This study contributes to answering the question of how growth companies choose their capital structures. In particular we analyze 1) how the debt ratio of growth companies is influenced by a comprehensive set of capital structure determinants and 2) if capital structure determinants differ between venture capital (VC) financed and non-VC financed companies. Our analysis uses a unique sample of 155 German growth companies during the time before their initial public offering (IPO). To analyze the dataset we employ fixed and random effects panel regression methods.

We provide evidence that ownership structure among venture capitalists and insiders, e.g. entrepreneurs and/or managers, significantly impacts the debt ratio of growth companies before the IPO but not thereafter. Higher relative equity shares of VC investors are accompanied by lower debt ratios. Most other capital structure determinants behave in the predicted way. While higher tangibility is associated with higher debt ratios, higher liquidity, profitability and risk imply lower levels of debt. Moreover, it appears that the relationship between the capital structure and company age, size and growth are different between companies financed with venture capital and those without.

Keywords: Capital structure · Venture capital · Financing policy · Growth companies

JEL Classification: G24 · G32 · L26

Prof. Dr. D. Grichnik (✉)
holds the Chair of Entrepreneurship at WHU – Otto Beisheim School of Management, Germany; Research Interests: Entrepreneurship, Entrepreneurial Finance; Contact: WHU – Otto Beisheim School of Management, Burgplatz 2, D-56179 Vallendar, Tel. +49 261 6509 - 261, E-Mail: grichnik@whu.edu, URL: www.whu.edu/unex

Prof. Dr. D. Schiereck (✉)
holds the Chair of Corporate Finance at the Technische Universität Darmstadt, Germany; Research Interests: Banking, Corporate Finance, Entrepreneurial Finance; Contact: TU Darmstadt, Hochschulstr. 1, D-64289 Darmstadt, Tel. + +49 (0)6151-16-4489, E-Mail: schiereck@bwl.tu-darmstadt.de, URL: www.prof-schiereck.de

Dr. A. Wenzel (✉)
was research assistant at the University Witten/Herdecke, E-Mail: wenzel_andreas@web.de.

1 Introduction

The venture capital boom during the 1990s has massively attracted the interest of the academic entrepreneurial finance community. As a consequence, a remarkable amount of both theoretic and empirical work has been carried out on the financing of newly founded and growing enterprises. Among the most heavily researched topics (Denis 2004) were the types of financial contracts used by venture capitalists (Admati/Pfleiderer 1994), the venture capital (VC) process (Gompers 1995, Bascha/Walz 2001 and Tykvová 2003), the performance of venture-backed firms (Brav/Gompers 1997), the relationship between VC investors and founders and/or management (Lerner 1995, Gompers 1999) and the characteristics of the VC funds themselves (Sahlman 1990). However, the question of how firms in the venture capital area choose their capital structures, has received only very little scientific attention, even though the capital structure puzzle (Myers/Majluf 1984, Myers 1984) is one of the classic and most fundamental topics of financial management and theory. The understanding of capital structure choice of growth companies (i.e. beyond start-up phase) is underdeveloped and except for mainly descriptive studies there are no empirical analyses available for Germany. Coevally, VC financing and the number of IPOs are growing again since 2005 after several "quiet" years following the burst of the New Economy-bubble. Even though in the current economic crisis, the question remains of fundamental interest, how growth firms chose their capital structure.

A company's financing decision is often termed as one of the most severe entrepreneurial decisions. This holds especially true for entrepreneurs of fast-growing young companies: Those entrepreneurial firms adjust their capital basis each time they have to finance company growth from external sources. Thus optimal financing and capital structure decisions are a permanent challenge for the management offering some freedom of design when selecting between different debt and equity suppliers. This challenge becomes even more obvious during periods of significantly changing market conditions like the current financial crisis where the easy access to debt capital of earlier times is more restricted und equity ratios gain higher importance.

Additionally, entrepreneurial firms feature some special characteristics which might restrict financial decisions, especially in times of an ongoing financial crisis. First, entrepreneurial firms compared to established large companies are often less diversified with their products, technologies, suppliers and customers, implying a higher default risk for potential investors. Second, young growth firms compared to established firms have a shorter track record and their business model often relies more heavily on implicit knowledge of the entrepreneurs. This increases the risk for investors because of less transparency and higher transactions cost to gather more information about the entrepreneurial team and the product market potential. Third, the valuation function of the public capital market is missing and hampers the ongoing assessment of the developing new business model. Thus, high-potential ventures face severe problems in financing their growth strategies. Nevertheless, empirical studies focusing on entrepreneurial financial behavior are seldom, German fast-growing entrepreneurial firms have hardly been object of an empirical study so far.

This paper addresses this research gap in entrepreneurial finance explicitly by investigating the relationship between VC financing and capital structure choice in entrepreneurial, fast-growing companies. In particular, we examine how the presence of VC financing affects the debt ratio and how the impact of other capital structure determinants – e.g. firm size, firm age, profitability – on the debt ratio differs between VC backed and non-VC backed firms. Since much of the VC related literature has focused on start-up companies, we turn our attention to companies that have already passed the first stage of their life cycle and that are now in the growth phase. We study a panel data set consisting of financial statement and ownership information over a seven year examination window on 155 firms that performed an initial public offering (IPO) on Germany's Neuer Markt between 1997 and 2000. This period is characterized by comparably attractive conditions for issuing equity. With respect to the ongoing financial crisis and the threat of a credit crunch we expect similar comparably attractive conditions for equity issues in the near future. Growth companies in need of additional financial resources might find only very limited access to new debt financing and therefore decide to go public and broaden the equity basis. However, the grown relative attractiveness of equity financing from external sources does not finally induce a judgment about the absolute attractiveness. It remains the possibility to completely resist from external financing and to decide for deferral of further investments.

Our findings suggest that VC involvement has a strong, direct effect on the capital structure choice of growth companies before the IPO whereas this effect vanishes as soon as shareholdings become widely dispersed. While the principal participation of VC investors implies lower debt ratios, their relative share of equity is positively correlated with the use of debt financing. This pattern implies a non-monotonistic functional relationship which can be considered to be strange. The indirect impact of venture capital on financing policy via other capital structure determinants, i.e. company size and age, tangibility, liquidity, profitability, growth, risk and taxes, can also be detected at an aggregate level. However, the evidence is scattered and not fully conclusive, which makes it difficult to interpret those findings.

The remainder of the paper is organized as follows. The second section provides an overview of the empirical research on capital structure in entrepreneurial firms. Section 3 describes the underlying hypotheses and theoretical reasoning. Section 4 presents the data sample and methodology. Section 5 contains the empirical results and discussion while section 6 summarizes the findings and concludes.

2 Background: Capital Structure of Entrepreneurial Firms

As stated above young high-growth firms differ from established firms in some important finance related characteristics such as stability of capital structure, diversification, information transparency, and access to capital markets. Therefore, traditional capital structure theories as trade-off and pecking order theory have uncertain explanation value for those entrepreneurial firms which can be shown by some empirical studies about IPO-firms in the US. Taking this as a starting point this study goes beyond classical capital structure choice to identify determinants of capital structure decisions in young entrepreneurial firms with high-growth potential exposed during an IPO.

Thus, the first focus of the literature review is concerned with a subcategory of studies regarding companies that are already beyond the start-up phase and have performed an initial public offering. Helwege and Liang (1996) analyze the incremental financial decisions of a sample of US-firms that has performed an IPO in order to test the validity of the two main competing schools of thoughts in capital structure theory – the trade-off theory and the pecking order theory (Harris/Raviv 1991). On the one hand, the static trade-off theory predicts that companies will always gradually adjust towards an optimal capital structure ratio. This target ratio results from weighing the costs and benefits of debt vs. equity financing, which are themselves functions of a set of determining parameters, i.e. the capital structure determinants. The dynamic version of the trade-off theory takes into account that realized debt ratios might actually never match optimal levels due to the existence of adjustment costs. However, this does not invalidate the directional impact of changes in capital structure determinants on the mix between debt and equity (Fischer et al. 1989). On the other hand the pecking order theory proclaims that there is no well-defined optimal debt ratio. Debt ratios change when there is an imbalance between net internal cash flow and real investment opportunities. Highly profitable firms with limited investment opportunities retain profits to lower debt ratios. Firms whose investment opportunities exceed internally generated funds borrow externally until their debt capacity is exhausted. Changes in debt ratios are driven by the need for funds, not by the attempt to reach an optimal capital structure (Myers 1984).

The estimation results of Helwege and Liang (1996) are not consistent with the pecking order theory, which leads the authors to conclude that the trade-off theory is indeed capable of explaining – at least partially – the financing behavior of growing, entrepreneurial firms. With regard to VC financing, they find that venture-backing does not have a significant influence on whether firms issue equity or debt. Using a comprehensive sample of German firms that have completed an IPO on the Neuer Markt, Audretsch and Lehmann (2003) analyze the determinants of VC financing. Compared to the other studies the causality is reversed, since VC financing is the dependent variable and the debt ratio one of the independent variables in the regression. They find that both the relative share and principal existence of VC financing are negatively correlated with the amount of debt financing.

Further empirical work on the capital structure of entrepreneurial firms can be broadly divided into two groups, one using descriptive analyses and the other employing regression techniques.

A typical example of the first category is Berger and Udell (1998) who describe the evolution of the mixture of debt and equity financing over the growth cycle of companies. Their descriptive, empirical analyses are carried out using detailed data on financing sources for small businesses in the United States. They show that the mix of financing sources as well as the capital structure of firms change significantly as they grow in size and age. Bessler and Kurth (2004) analyze the ratio of book equity to total assets for 313 companies that went public on Germany's Neuer Markt between 1997 and 2000 for the period from two years prior to the IPO to the year thereafter. As expected, the average equity ratio is highest in the IPO-year. Furthermore they discover that the frequency distributions of equity ratios differ significantly between the year before the IPO and the IPO-year itself; the observed equity ratios cover the complete theoretical range from 0% to 100%. Based on these findings they conclude that there cannot be a unique, optimal capital structure for IPOs of growth companies but that the relative usage of different financing sources rather depends on the characteristics and life-cycle stage of the individual companies. At first sight this statement could appear to be a contradiction to the theory of optimal capital structure, e.g. as potential evidence against dynamic trade-off vs. pecking order. However it is not, since the theory explicitly asserts that the optimal capital structure of any company at any given time is a function of several company-specific parameters, the so-called capital structure determinants.

Wenzel (2006) provides similar findings and a detailed analysis on capital structure determinants to test capital structure theories such as pecking order theory and trade-off theory. The following study is based upon that analysis and dataset and extends the study with a new focus on ownership structure before and after the IPO of young growth firms with new empirical insights. Therefore, also the literature background and discussion provides a broader view on the phenomenon of venture capital involvement and capital structure choice. Some general findings included also in Wenzel (2006) are explicitly marked in this study.

Our study is part of the group of empirical works with the objective to uncover the relationships between the observed capital structure ratios and their determinants by means of regression techniques with different data sets. This research can be classified by the type of company under investigation. Chittenden et al. (1996) and Michaelas et al. (1999) analyze the impact of a broad set of capital structure determinants including profitability, growth rate, asset structure, size, age and several proxy variables on the book value-based debt ratio of 3,500 small and medium-sized enterprises in the UK. The main difference between the two studies lies in the data sample and empirical method employed. While Chittenden et al. (1996) employ static cross-sectional regressions on their sample of firms, Michaelas et al. (1999) run fixed-effects regressions on their panel data set, which contains ten years of data for each firm in the sample. The latter approach is clearly advantageous due to the significantly increased sample size and the resulting increased power of significance tests. The authors document that profitability, growth rate, asset structure and age have a statistically significant impact on the debt ratio. Chittenden et al. (1996) show that access to public capital markets not only impacts the debt ratio directly but also influences the relationship of all other capital structure determinants on the dependent variable. Michaelas et al. (1999) include the effective tax rate and non-debt tax shields as additional explanatory variables but do not find any significant relationship with the total debt ratio.

Cassar (2001) and Huyghebaert and Van de Gucht (2002) focus on the determining factors of the capital structure of start-up companies. By means of a sample of Australian firms Cassar (2001) provides evidence that company size is positively related to leverage while growth prospects show a negative impact. Huyghebaert and Van de Gucht (2002) estimate a simultaneous equation model for a sample of Belgian start-ups. The analyzed dimensions of capital structure are debt ratio, proportion of bank debt and debt maturity. The authors construct proxy variables for adverse selection, moral hazard and control rents by combining firm, industry and ownership data. Concerning leverage, they show that it is negatively related to the extent of adverse selection and moral hazard problems and to control rents enjoyed by the founder.

The above survey of prior research on the capital structure of entrepreneurial firms documents that the empirical evidence with regard to the relationship between VC financing and capital structure choice is rather scarce and partly inconsistent. Börner et al. (2009) show in detail the inconsistency of prior empirical findings for capital structure determinants. E.g., although Sogorb-Mira (2005) and Heymann et al. (2008) support a significantly positive effect of company size on the debt ratio of the firms, Rajan and Zingales (2005) cannot confirm this finding. Furthermore, most examinations on entrepreneurial companies can only use few independent variables to explain debt ratios because of the limited (amount of) variables contained in the analyzed databases. This study contributes to closing the research gap by analyzing the capital structure choice of German growth companies with a comprehensive set of regressors before and after their IPO.

3 Hypotheses: Capital Structure Determinants

We use the book value of debt divided by the book value of total assets as a measure of capital structure and as dependent variable in the regressions. Market value-based capital structure measures could only be used for the time after the IPO. Doing this would however restrict the comparability of pre-IPO and post-IPO estimates.

Our choice of capital structure determinants – firm's age, size, tangible assets, liquidity, profitability, growth, operating risk, tax rates, non-debt tax shields – is guided by the existing empirical literature (Titman/Wessels 1988, Rajan/Zingales 1995, Chittenden et al. 1996, Michaelas et al. 1999, Frank/Goyal 2003, López-Gracia/Sogorb-Mira 2008, Heymann et al. 2008). Furthermore, we include ownership structure in order to reflect the impact of VC financing on capital structure choice.

Age: Company age can be interpreted as an indicator of the extent of asymmetric information between management and external investors (Berger/Udell 1998). According to the regular version of the pecking order theory (Myers/Majluf 1984, Myers 1984) firms issue the safest security first when external funds are needed. For established firms debt is safer than equity, because its value is relatively less dependent on information about the company than equity. As companies grow older and more information becomes available the relative uncertainty of equity vs. debt shrinks, which should in turn lead to a lower debt ratio. However, these propositions of the classic version of the pecking order could be reversed for young growth firms that are privately held (Garmaise 1997, Voulgaris et al. 2004). The ties between company insiders and equity investors are typically much closer than those to creditors, which implies that equity securities should be less undervalued than debt and thus "safer" to issue for young, privately held firms. When companies go public, equity ownership typically becomes much more dispersed which loosens the ties to equity investors. This in turn implies a reversion back to regular pecking-order-behavior. Therefore, we expect a negative relationship between company age and debt ratio before the IPO (Sogorb-Mira 2005, Zoppa/MacMahon 2002) and a positive relationship thereafter (López-Gracia/Sogorb-Mira 2008).

H1a: The age of a company is negatively related to its level of debt before the IPO.
H1b: The age of a company is positively related to its level of debt after the IPO.

Size: Expected bankruptcy costs decrease with increasing company size, since both the probability of bankruptcy and the relative share of bankruptcy costs of company value decrease. Lower expected bankruptcy costs make a company more attractive as debtor so that we expect higher debt ratios for larger companies (Robichek/Myers 1966, Hirshleifer

1970). Additional support for this hypothesis comes from the agency theory of capital structure. Principal-agent-problems induced by the assumption of debt, i.e. underinvestment (Myers 1977) and asset substitution (Jensen/Meckling 1976), are more pronounced in smaller companies. Creditors of larger companies dispose of more and better information to prevent and/or resolve such conflicts than those of smaller companies (Sogorb-Mira 2005, Zoppa/MacMahon 2002, Hall et al. 2004).

H2: The size of a company is positively related to its level of debt.

Tangibility: It is easier for lenders to establish the value of tangible than intangible assets, because typically there is more asymmetric information about the value of the latter (Myers/Majluf 1984). Moreover, it is highly likely that in the face of probable bankruptcy intangible assets like goodwill will rapidly disappear thus diminishing the net worth of a firm and further raising its bankruptcy probability. Expected bankruptcy costs are therefore positively correlated with the relative share of intangible assets. Furthermore, issuing debt secured by fixed assets reduces moral hazard in form of the asset substitution problem (Smith/Warner 1979, Smith/Wakeman 1985). Hence, we argue that firms with relatively more tangible assets have a higher capacity for raising debt and will thus display higher debt ratios (Rajan/Zingales 1995, Autore/Kovacs 2004, Heymann et al. 2008).

H3: Firm debt is positively related to the volume of firm tangible assets.

Liquidity: By definition, the value of dynamic growth companies consists to a large degree of future investment opportunities. Other things equal companies can improve their ability to actually take advantage of those opportunities by increasing financial flexibility (Cornell/Shapiro 1988). Debt financing usually implies fixed periodic payments and very often the provision of collateral. In contrast to equity, debt markedly restrains financial flexibility. We therefore hypothesize that growth companies will either retain liquidity internally to fund future projects or to pay down debt in order to increase financial flexibility. Hence, higher liquidity should be associated with lower debt levels. The logic of the agency theory that higher cash levels increase the threat of overinvestment and should therefore be countered by the assumption of higher debt levels (Jensen/Meckling 1976) does not apply to growth companies, since they are typically cash-constrained and have sufficient profitable investment opportunities (López-Gracia/Sogorb-Mira 2008).

H4: Firm debt is negatively related to the volume of firm liquidity.

Profitability: The reasoning with regard to profitability is similar to the logic concerning liquidity. Growth companies retain profits in order to increase financial flexibility and become less dependent on external financing. This is also in line with the classic version of the pecking order theory, which asserts that companies only access external financing sources when all internal funds are exhausted (Myers/Majluf 1984). The classic trade-off theory proclaims that more profitable firms should assume more debt in order to exploit tax shields to the maximum possible extent (Modigliani/Miller 1963, Baxter 1967, Kraus/Litzenberger 1973, Kim 1978, Heymann et al. 2008). We deem financial flexibility to be more important for growth companies than tax considerations (Cornell/Shapiro 1988), which are mostly a concern for mature companies. Therefore we argue that higher profitability should imply a relatively higher share of equity financing.

H5: There is a negative relationship between debt ratio and firm profitability.

Growth: In previous paragraphs we have argued that strongly growing companies prefer to keep as much financial flexibility as possible by retaining funds internally. If internal liquidity is exhausted, external funds must be raised to finance further growth. Like discussed in the context of company age, the pecking order predicts that companies access debt financing first before additional equity is raised. Consequently, we argue that this reasoning is reversed while companies are still in private ownership due to strong ties between management and shareholders. In analogy to company age we thus predict a negative relationship between growth and debt ratio before the IPO (Heymann et al. 2008, López-Gracia/Sogorb-Mira 2008) and a positive correlation thereafter (Cassar/Holmes 2003, Sánchez-Vidal/Martín-Ugedo 2005).

H6a: The growth of a company is negatively related to its debt ratio before the IPO.
H6b: The growth of a company is positively related to its debt ratio after the IPO.

Risk: The operating risk of a company can be regarded as a proxy of bankruptcy probability. The more risky the business operations the less certain external investors can be that they will eventually be able to recoup their capital. Higher operating risk should therefore be associated with lower debt ratios (Castanias 1983, López-Gracia/Sogorb-Mira 2008).

H7: Operating risk is negatively related to the firm's debt ratio.

Tax rate: According to the trade-off theory high corporate tax rates enable companies to increase total company value via tax shields (Modigliani/Miller 1963, López-Gracia/Sogorb-Mira 2008). However, as already laid out above in the context of profitability, tax shields are only of inferior importance to growth companies. Furthermore, earnings of growth companies can be very volatile, which makes tax shields much less attractive. We therefore expect the debt ratio not to show any significant correlation to tax rates.

H8: Tax rates are not significantly related to the level of debt.

Non-debt tax shields: DeAngelo and Masulis (1980) have derived that non-debt tax shields, e.g. depreciation and amortization, are substitutes for debt-induced tax shields. All other things equal, companies with higher depreciation and amortization charges should therefore have less debt on the balance sheet (Heymann et al. 2008, López-Gracia/Sogorb-Mira 2008). However, we do not believe that tax considerations play a major role in capital structure decisions of growth companies. In addition, the theoretical logic of DeAngelo and Masulis (1980) is not undisputed. Higher non-debt tax shields in the form of depreciation charges could also be a result of a higher proportion of fixed assets, which in turn would make debt financing more attractive. In summary, we expect the debt ratio to be neutral with regard to non-debt tax shields.

H9: Non-debt tax shields are not significantly related to the firm debt.

The following group of hypotheses focuses on

Ownership structure: In the context of ownership structure we analyze separately how VC and insider involvement in financing affect debt ratios. Concerning the participation of VC investors, two aspects need to be taken into account. First, capital structure choice can be affected by whether or not a portion of the share capital is provided by VC investors. Second, their relative equity share can also have an impact on the debt level. As argued earlier, ties to equity investors might be stronger than those to creditors for growth companies that have not yet gone public. If sufficient financing capacity is available, privately held growth companies therefore first approach potential shareholders with the request for additional capital. In contrast to founders, friends and family, which typically only provide seed capital, VC investors can make sizeable investments (Berger/Udell 1998) so that companies need to rely on debt to a much lesser extent. This is considered to hold true although the financing volume of the VC investor can be seen as an endogenous variable which cannot be unconfinedly interpreted as a capital structure determinant. Companies that have gone public and can access capital markets are to a much lesser extent reliant on financing from private equity sources or banks. Therefore we expect companies with VC involvement to display lower debt ratios than companies without VC financing before the IPO. For the time after the IPO we do not expect a significant impact of VC participation on the debt ratio.

H10a: High-growth firms with VC involvement have a low level of pre-IPO debt.
H10b: VC involvement is not significantly related to the post-IPO level of debt.

Concerning the relative equity share of VC investors we expect a positive relationship to the debt ratio pre-IPO and the lack of significant impact thereafter. The reasoning is twofold. First, VC investors having the goal to maximize their return on investment can achieve this by maximizing their relative equity share. In the case of additional financing needs profit-maximizing VC investors would therefore prefer the borrowing of debt over additional equity, since the latter would dilute their rate of return. Second, higher equity shares of VC investors should increase the confidence of other financial intermediaries, e.g. banks, to participate in financing. This line of reasoning would support the point that higher relative equity shares of VC investors are compatible with higher debt ratios. After the IPO those effects lose significance.

H11a: Higher relative equity shares of VC investors are positively related to the firm's pre-IPO debt ratio.
H11b: VC investors shareholding is not significantly related to the firm post-IPO debt.

Theoretical considerations on capital structure decisions in entrepreneurial companies (Anderson/Nyborg 2001, Dewatripont et al. 2002) argue that company success is linked to the motivation of the founder and/or management team. Their equity share can act as a very powerful incentive in this context. Therefore relative equity shares of insiders are deemed to be positively correlated with debt ratios. We adopt this reasoning as hypothesis for the time before the initial public offering. Company insiders typically divest major portions of their shareholdings in the course of the IPO, which substantially weakens their influence for the time thereafter. We do therefore not expect an effect of insider shareholdings on post-IPO capital structure.

H12a: Equity shares of insiders are positively related to the firm's pre-IPO debt ratio.
H12b: Insider shareholding is not significantly related to the firm post-IPO debt.

Table 1 summarizes the hypothesized relationships between capital structure determinants and the debt ratio.

Table 1. Overview of capital structure determinants and hypotheses
The book value of debt divided by the book value of total assets is used as a measure of capital structure and as dependent variable in the regressions. For the descriptions of the independent variables see Table 3. Note: + = positively related; – = negatively related; o = not significantly related.

Hypotheses	Capital structure determinant	Hypothesized relationship to debt ratio		
		Pre-IPO	Post-IPO	Overall
H1	Age	–	+	
H2	Size	+	+	+
H3	Tangibility	+	+	+
H4	Liquidity	–	–	–
H5	Profitability	–	–	–
H6	Growth	–	+	
H7	Risk	–	–	–
H8	Tax rate	o	o	o
H9	Non-debt tax shields	o	o	o
H10	Participation of VC investors	–	o	
H11	Equity share of VC investors	+	o	
H12	Equity share of insiders	+	o	

4 Data and Methodology

As already indicated we focus our analyses on growth companies, which can be regarded as a subset of entrepreneurial companies according to the life cycle theory (Churchill/ Lewis 1983, Walker 1989, Hanks et al. 1993). As a starting point, we take all companies that have performed an IPO on Germany's Neuer Markt, the former special growth segment of Deutsche Börse AG, between 1997 and 2002. By definition of Deutsche Börse AG, the market segment 'Neuer Markt' was only allowed as a listing platform for growth companies. However, the classification was not formally derived but showed some qualitative evaluations. The rules and regulations of the Neuer Markt stipulated that all listed companies must submit complete financial statements including profit and loss statement, balance sheet and cash flow statement. Moreover, companies are obliged to include three years of pre-IPO financial statements in their issue prospectuses. This provides us with the opportunity to generate financial statement data both for the time of private as well as public ownership.

In order to avoid distortions of results due to different accounting practices or regulatory influences on balance sheet structures we restrict our sample to companies incorporated in Germany and exclude financial institutions. An additional sample selection criterion is the availability of three years of financial statements before and after the IPO resulting in seven years of financial data for each company. Due to these restrictions the initial population of 330 IPOs on the Neuer Markt is narrowed down to 155 companies in the final sample. The included growth firms are classified by Deutsche Börse AG due to their above average growth expectations and with respect to industry classification. Since

Table 2. IPOs on Germany's Neuer Markt by calendar year

Calendar year	1997	1998	1999	2000	2001	2002
Total # of IPOs on Neuer Markt	12	41	132	133	11	1
thereof in sample	*5*	*24*	*60*	*66*	*0*	*0*

the calculation of some explanatory variables requires data from two periods 930 firm-year-observations enter into the regression estimates. Table 2 depicts the distribution of all Neuer Markt-IPOs and of the subset of companies that entered into our sample by calendar year.

As a side effect, the data restrictions lead to a selection of and a concentration on IPO firms which have longer track records with more reliable business models and therefore higher survival rates than average going publics at the Neuer Markt. Additionally the period under consideration is characterized by comparably attractive conditions for issuing equity. With respect to the ongoing financial crisis and the threat of a credit crunch we expect similar comparably attractive conditions for equity issues in the near future. Growth companies in need of additional financial resources might find only very limited access to new debt financing and therefore decide to go public and broaden the equity basis, even when the increased relative attractiveness is considered to be expensive in absolute terms. Both aspects together offer good confidence that the following results are of general importance.

Besides data from balance sheet, profit and loss and cash flow statements we also use data on the ownership structure of the companies before and after the IPO. This data on ownership structure is not available on an annual basis but only for the time before the IPO and thereafter resulting in two data points per ownership variable and company. Due to the fact that companies were not restricted to use uniform accounting standards the sample includes financial statements in three different standards: German accounting rules, IAS (today called IFRS) and US-GAAP. Accounting-dummy variables are introduced in the regressions to control for any impact on the debt ratio.

In order to test the hypothesized relationships between the debt ratio and the capital structure determinants the latter are operationalized via explanatory variables. Table 3 describes the construction of all explanatory variables. In addition, we include dummy variables for the year relative to the IPO, the industry, the calendar year of the respective observation and the form of company foundation (new start-up vs. equity carve out).

Table 4 depicts the mean and standard deviation of the dependent variable and the explanatory variables by year relative to the IPO. As expected, the debt ratio is lowest in the IPO-year due to the massive influx of additional equity capital. This is also reflected in the liquidity ratio, which reaches on average 45% of total assets in the IPO-year. The high standard deviation of company age relative to the mean highlights the substantial age spread in the sample. The oldest company in the sample was founded 77 years prior to the going public. However, this number does not necessarily contradict the classification as a growth company, since even mature companies can re-enter the growth phase by a radical change in strategic direction or by major product innovations.

The increase in means of size and growth variables over time shows that, on average, companies follow a steady growth path throughout the period under investigation. The

Table 3. Overview of explanatory variables

Variable	Description	Type
Age		
AGE	Number of years since foundation	Real
Size		
TA	Natural log of total assets	Real
REV	Natural log of net revenues	Real
Tangibility		
FIX	Property, plant and equipment divided by total assets	Percent
INV	Inventory divided by total assets	Percent
AR	Accounts receivable divided by total assets	Percent
Liquidity		
LIQU	Liquid assets of previous year divided by total assets of previous year	Percent
FCF	Free cash flow divided by total assets	Percent
Profitability		
PROF	Operating result divided by total assets	Percent
Growth		
G_TA	Annual growth rate of total assets	Percent
G_REV	Annual growth rate of net revenues	Percent
Risk		
RISK	Standard deviation of growth rate of operating profit calculated over all periods	Real
Tax rate		
TAX	Adjusted tax rate (set equal to zero if either less than zero or greater than one)	Percent
Non-debt tax shields		
NDTS	Depreciation & amortization divided by total assets	Percent
Ownership structure		
VC	Existence of VC financing	Binary (1-yes; 0-no)
SH_VC	Relative equity share of VC investors	Percent
SH_INS	Relative equity share of insiders	Percent

decline in all tangible asset ratios post-IPO is mirrored both by the rising liquidity ratio as well as by an increasing volume of intangible assets. The latter is not directly documented in the above statistics but the finding is implied by the increasing amount of depreciation and amortization relative to total assets.

As already mentioned, data on ownership structure is not available on an annual basis but only for the time before the IPO and thereafter resulting in two data points per ownership variable and company. Venture capital investors contributed to the financing of 65 out of the 155 companies in the sample. The average equity share of VC investors shrank from 32% pre-IPO to 17% post-IPO. The initial public offering also caused a decline in the equity share of company insiders, from 62% pre-IPO to 44% thereafter. Table 5 displays the frequency distribution of equity shares of VC investors and insiders before and after the IPO. From the constant number of companies without VC involvement, it can be seen that none of the VC investors has completely divested of its equity holdings in

Table 4. Descriptive analysis of variables

Period	Mean							Standard deviation						
	-3	-2	-1	0	1	2	3	-3	-2	-1	0	1	2	3
Debt ratio														
DR (in %)	83	85	78	29	36	44	49	42	64	115	17	18	21	24
Age														
AGE	11.6	12.6	13.6	14.6	15.6	16.6	17.6	10.6	10.6	10.6	10.6	10.6	10.6	10.6
Size														
TA	16	20	28	119	137	146	212	26	32	41	564	493	485	962
REV	21	28	37	56	85	105	117	37	57	82	118	147	189	259
Tangibility														
FIX (in %)	17.7	17.3	16.3	9.4	11.4	12.9	12.8	19.0	17.3	16.4	11.0	10.7	12.4	13.1
INV (in %)	13.6	12.9	12.4	6.6	8.2	8.4	8.6	16.8	16.2	16.1	8.8	10.6	10.2	11.2
AR (in %)	26.5	27.3	24.2	14.4	17.9	17.5	17.8	18.9	19.4	17.2	10.5	11.8	10.9	11.6
Liquidity														
LIQU (in %)	14.1	14.6	19.7	45.1	27.2	23.3	22.5	17.0	17.3	22.3	23.2	21.0	21.4	20.9
FCF (in %)	-10.3	-11.3	-9.1	-24.5	-22.4	-12.2	-4.8	57.2	42.9	24.6	21.6	27.3	22.8	23.3
Profitability														
PROF (in %)	-2.4	0.2	5.8	0.5	-10.6	-20.5	-15.6	50.8	53.9	22.7	13.1	31.1	46.9	32.6
Growth														
G_TA (in %)	na	156	427	49	10	4	93	na	563	662	134	90	128	291
G_REV (in %)	na	57	154	69	40	5	107	na	112	767	86	136	59	367
Risk														
RISK (in %)	10.2	10.2	10.2	10.2	10.2	10.2	10.2	24.9	24.9	24.9	24.9	24.9	24.9	24.9
Tax rate														
TAX (in %)	32.6	35.2	33.9	31.2	26.2	20.0	16.2	26.5	26.1	23.3	24.7	22.7	23.0	21.5
Non-debt tax shields														
NDTS (in %)	8.8	9.3	7.6	3.9	9.9	16.1	15.6	8.6	13.0	8.6	4.5	18.9	33.4	28.6

course of the initial public offering. In contrast the number of companies without shareholdings of company insiders has increased from 8 pre-IPO to 9 post-IPO.

The aim of this study is to investigate the relationship between capital structure and VC financing. To this end we estimate multivariate regression models with the debt ratio as dependent variable. The panel character of our data allows us to use fixed and random effects panel regression methods. According to Baltagi (1996) the greatest advantage of panel data is that they allow control for individual heterogeneity. To verify the character – fixed or random – of the unobservable individual effects, the Hausman's (1978) specification test can be employed. A disadvantage of the Hausman-test is however its relatively low power and the problem that the test statistic can often not be calculated. If autocorrelation and/or heteroskedasticity are detected, we use robust estimators of coefficient covariance matrices in order to be able to conduct valid significance tests. Specifically, we use the robust variance estimator proposed by White (1984).

Table 5. Frequency distribution of equity share of VC investors and insiders before and after the IPO

Equity share	VC investors		Insiders	
	Pre-IPO	Post-IPO	Pre-IPO	Post-IPO
0%	90	90	8	9
>0% – 10%	4	20	7	11
>10% – 20%	19	22	9	12
>20% – 30%	12	15	11	10
>30% – 40%	13	5	5	15
>40% – 50%	10	2	12	20
>50% – 60%	1	1	14	28
>60% – 70%	2	0	13	35
>70% – 80%	2	0	19	15
>80% – 90%	2	0	17	0
>90% – 100%	0	0	40	0
Total	155	155	155	155

5 Findings

This section is structured according to the two main research questions. In the first subsection we analyze how VC financing affects companies' debt ratio. In the second subsection we turn our attention to how VC financed companies differ from non-VC financed firms with regard to the impact of other capital structure determinants.

5.1 The impact of VC financing on capital structure

The results of the regression of the debt ratio on the set of explanatory variables are depicted in Table 6. The regression is carried out for three different time frames: all years of the dataset, the time before the IPO and the time after the IPO. The firm effects are alternatively specified as fixed effects (FE) and random effects (RE) for each period. In the case of autocorrelated and/or heteroskedastic residuals robust standard error estimates are used.

As can be seen from the results of the F-tests, all regressions except for the RE-regression pre-IPO turn out to be highly significant. As expected the R2 within is maximized by the FE-estimations while the values of R2 between and R2 overall are higher in the RE-regressions. The Hausman-test statistic can only be calculated for the post-IPO period. Here, the null hypothesis of higher efficiency of the RE model specification (REM specification) can be rejected at the 1 percent level of significance. The documented R2 in Table 6 reach a level which is slightly higher than in comparable recent studies on VC financed vs. non-VC financed firms (Masulis/Nahata 2008).

In face of the highly significant F-test for the fixed effects regression pre-IPO only one coefficient – the growth rate of total assets – turns out to be significantly different from zero. The negative sign supports the hypothesis that higher growth before the IPO implies lower debt ratios. Despite the insignificant F-statistic the REM specification for the time before the IPO results in four significant coefficients. The negative coefficient of the variable AGE supports the hypothesized relationship, while the negative impact of total assets on the debt ratio contradicts the respective hypothesis. However, the latter makes sense if asset growth is mainly driven by rising equity and not matched by simultaneous growth of operations in the same order of magnitude. Furthermore, in line with hypotheses, the debt ratio does not seem to be influenced by tax rates or non-debt tax shields. Most importantly however, for the focus of this study, the coefficients of the two variables related to VC financing show the expected signs. Companies with involvement of VC investors have significantly lower debt ratios than non-VC financed companies. Moreover, for companies with VC financing, the relative equity share of VC investors correlates positively with the extent of debt financing.

The estimation of the regression equation for the time after the IPO yields many more significant relationships than for the pre-IPO period, and most findings are in line with the expectations expressed by the hypotheses. The results regarding the variables on tangibility support the expected relationship. This is also true for the regressors on liquidity and profitability and for the findings with regard to revenue growth. Asset growth does not turn out to have a significant impact. The post-IPO estimates also provide evidence for the hypothesis that companies' operating risk negatively impacts the debt ratio. Only TAX shows a negative sign which contradicts the hypothesis of missing influence of tax-related parameters. If higher tax rates are a result of higher profitability, this would however support the pecking-order logic, which was followed in deriving the hypotheses on liquidity and profitability.

The aggregated results for the complete period under consideration underline once again the importance of VC. The value of the variable VC is significantly negative. Also, most of the other variables show expected signs.

Table 6. Panel regressions of all companies by subperiod
The book value of debt divided by the book value of total assets is used as a measure of capital structure and as dependent variable in the regressions. For the descriptions of the independent variables see Table 3. The regression is carried out for three different time frames: all years of the dataset, the time before the IPO and the time after the IPO. The firm effects are alternatively specified as fixed effects (FE) and random effects (RE) for each period. In case of autocorrelated and/or heteroskedastic residuals robust standard error estimates are used. Note: *, ** and ***, significant at the 10, 5 and 1 percent level respectively. Standard errors are in parentheses.

	Pre-IPO		Post-IPO		All periods	
Regression model	FEM	REM	FEM	REM	FEM	REM
Standard errors	Normal	White	White	White	Normal	White
# periods	2	2	3	3	6	6
# companies	155	155	154	154	155	155
# observations	304	305	461	461	917	917
Constant	-1.6431	1.1882**	1.3918**	0.7363**	0.6665	0.7354**
	(2.7389)	(0.5199)	(0.5462)	(0.2963)	(0.9504)	(0.3268)
AGE		-0.0070*		-0.0013		-0.0025*
		(0.0042)		(0.0012)		(0.0014)
TA	0.1729	-0.0835*	-0.0580	-0.0326	-0.0673	-0.0527**
	(0.2894)	(0.0464)	(0.0445)	(0.0259)	(0.0539)	(0.0207)
REV	0.1083	0.0680	-0.0307	0.0119	0.0111	0.0406
	(0.2709)	(0.0466)	(0.0415)	(0.0237)	(0.0585)	(0.0284)

Table 6 (continued)

Regression model Standard errors	Pre-IPO		Post-IPO		All periods	
	FEM Normal	REM White	FEM White	REM White	FEM Normal	REM White
FIX	0.2702	0.4274	0.0687	0.2002*	0.4888	0.3534**
	(1.2479)	(0.2828)	(0.2312)	(0.1134)	(0.3098)	(0.1784)
INV	-0.7020	0.0536	0.3344***	0.2600**	0.1539	0.0411
	(1.0978)	(0.2007)	(0.1273)	(0.1197)	(0.2936)	(0.1586)
AR	-0.9713	0.0120	0.3311*	0.3542***	0.1496	0.2729
	(1.0694)	(0.4585)	(0.1720)	(0.1231)	(0.2305)	(0.2971)
LIQU	1.2416	-0.0714	-0.0938	-0.1565***	-0.2534*	-0.2559*
	(0.7988)	(0.1681)	(0.0696)	(0.0590)	(0.1377)	(0.1345)
FCF	-0.5555	-0.4227	0.0472	0.0098	-0.1128	-0.1313
	(0.4253)	(0.4322)	(0.0660)	(0.0498)	(0.0981)	(0.1092)
PROF	-0.0028	-0.0864	-0.1600**	-0.1718***	-0.1561	-0.2252***
	(0.3643)	(0.2221)	(0.0708)	(0.0555)	(0.1028)	(0.0831)
G_TA	-0.0501*	-0.0161	-0.0115	-0.0056	-0.0050	-0.0059**
	(0.0255)	(0.0114)	(0.0124)	(0.0090)	(0.0063)	(0.0027)
G_REV	-0.0253	-0.0009	0.0221**	0.0150**	0.0008	0.0030*
	(0.0327)	(0.0144)	(0.0103)	(0.0072)	(0.0064)	(0.0018)
RISK		-0.0006		-0.0007**		-0.0007
		(0.0019)		(0.0004)		(0.0007)
TAX	0.0678	-0.2636	-0.0580*	-0.0665**	-0.0766	-0.1165
	(0.3436)	(0.2399)	(0.0330)	(0.0279)	(0.0963)	(0.0818)
NDTS	0.0141	-0.5493	-0.0886	-0.0840	-0.1103	-0.1771
	(1.4611)	(0.3596)	(0.0695)	(0.0541)	(0.1463)	(0.1139)
VC		-0.4460**		-0.0176		-0.1095**
		(0.2216)		(0.0445)		(0.0464)
SH_VC		0.6917*		-0.0565	-0.2351	0.0273
		(0.3724)		(0.1953)	(0.3697)	(0.1822)
SH_INS		0.2228		0.0244	0.2400	0.0941
		(0.2177)		(0.0752)	(0.2972)	(0.0867)
R^2 within	0.0941	0.0414	0.4658	0.4237	0.1956	0.1911
R^2 between	0.0098	0.1808	0.0748	0.4158	0.1252	0.2669
R^2 overall	0.0000	0.1250	0.1289	0.4172	0.1751	0.2114
F-test	1.536***	1.018	12.143***	8.883***	2.485***	5.528***
Hausman-test		na		82.880***		na

5.2 Capital structure determinants of VC financed vs. non-VC financed firms

This section sheds light on the question whether the influence of capital structure determinants on the debt ratio differs between companies with and without VC involvement. To analyze this issue we have multiplied the dummy variable VC with all other variables not related to ownership structure and introduced these multiplicative terms (interactive terms) as additional explanatory variables in the regression equation. Table 7 shows the resulting estimates by period and specification in analogy to the previous section.

Table 7. Panel regressions of all companies by subperiod with VC financing as interactive dummy variable
The book value of debt divided by the book value of total assets is used as a measure of capital structure and as dependent variable in the regressions. For the descriptions of the independent variables see Table 3. For VC involvement the dummy variable VC is multiplied with all other variables not related to ownership structure and these multiplicative terms are introduced as additional explanatory variables in the regression equation The regression is carried out for three different time frames: all years of the dataset, the time before the IPO and the time after the IPO. The firm effects are alternatively specified as fixed effects (FE) and random effects (RE) for each period. In case of autocorrelated and/or heteroskedastic residuals robust standard error estimates are used.
Note: *, ** and ***, significant at the 10, 5 and 1 percent level respectively. Standard errors are in parentheses.

Regression model	Pre-IPO		Post-IPO		All periods	
	FEM	REM	FEM	REM	FEM	REM
Standard errors	White	White	White	White	White	White
# periods	2	2	3	3	6	6
# companies	154	154	154	154	155	155
# observations	304	304	461	461	917	917
Constant	1.1290	2.4345	1.5453**	0.6787	1.0049	1.2022*
	4.6436	1.7384	0.7158	0.4857	0.6913	0.6581
AGE		-0.0046		-0.0029*		-0.0046**
		0.0045		0.0016		0.0018
VC*AGE		0.0034		0.0036*		0.0054**
		0.0067		0.0021		0.0026
TA	0.8448	-0.1403	-0.0359	-0.0175	-0.1427***	-0.0848**
	0.9571	0.0962	0.0606	0.0299	0.0483	0.0395
VC*TA	-1.0451	0.0980	-0.0613	-0.0377	0.1297*	0.0785
	0.9326	0.1456	0.0772	0.0424	0.0718	0.0711
REV	-0.6700	0.0298	-0.0714	0.0106	0.0105	0.0399
	0.6812	0.1018	0.0943	0.0377	0.0988	0.0467
VC*REV	0.7093	0.0135	0.0577	0.0054	-0.0108	-0.0162
	0.6836	0.1096	0.1020	0.0480	0.0910	0.0463
FIX	-0.5234	-0.0418	-0.0460	0.2062	0.0201	0.3025
	1.9837	0.6256	0.3373	0.1630	0.7453	0.2058
VC*FIX	1.8370	1.0395	0.4085	0.1573	0.8853	0.2778
	2.1940	0.7843	0.4442	0.1866	0.7684	0.2099
INV	-5.7878*	-0.2748	0.4047**	0.2837	-0.0590	-0.1232
	3.0131	0.5600	0.1926	0.1728	0.4542	0.2381
VC*INV	5.6599*	0.5623	-0.1712	0.0713	0.3160	0.3999
	3.0667	0.5639	0.3561	0.2397	0.4279	0.2503
AR	-2.0984	-0.3205	0.0978	0.1623	-0.3763	0.1633
	2.1430	0.9668	0.2400	0.1193	1.2206	0.5102
VC*AR	2.0256	0.4140	0.4974	0.4410*	1.0680	0.2989
	2.2171	0.9721	0.3586	0.2528	1.2782	0.5306
LIQUID	1.1750	0.4318	-0.1089	-0.2094**	-0.2504	-0.2989*
	1.6072	0.5691	0.0975	0.0853	0.2059	0.1613
VC*LIQUID	-0.8303	-0.4677	0.0276	0.1101	0.1549	0.1526
	1.6293	0.5699	0.1275	0.1055	0.2076	0.1456
FCF	-0.6615	-1.4733	0.0123	-0.0331	-0.2178	-0.2451
	0.9665	1.4036	0.0481	0.0458	0.2527	0.2161

Table 7 (continued)

Regression model Standard errors	Pre-IPO		Post-IPO		All periods	
	FEM White	REM White	FEM White	REM White	FEM White	REM White
VC*FCF	0.7542 1.0344	1.5011 1.3654	0.0676 0.1098	0.0986 0.0867	0.2485 0.2430	0.2338 0.2146
PROF	0.4459 1.6785	-0.1611 0.9173	-0.1999 0.1272	-0.2272** 0.0918	-0.0248 0.1876	-0.3413 0.2921
VC*PROF	-0.7336 1.6885	-0.1589 0.9099	0.0514 0.1344	0.0592 0.0985	-0.2640 0.1773	0.0560 0.2775
G_TA	-1.3739** 0.6011	0.2236 0.1619	-0.0390** 0.0192	-0.0157 0.0119	0.0006 0.0044	0.0027 0.0070
VC*G_TA	1.3731** 0.5991	-0.2375 0.1667	0.0468** 0.0229	0.0232 0.0173	-0.0034 0.0053	-0.0098 0.0104
G_REV	0.0001 0.2357	-0.2584 0.2563	0.0455 0.0315	0.0188 0.0175	-0.0311 0.0442	-0.0053 0.0255
VC*G_REV	0.0017 0.2362	0.2703 0.2605	-0.0320 0.0329	-0.0092 0.0193	0.0322 0.0458	0.0095 0.0276
RISK		-0.0013 0.0030		-0.0014 0.0009		-0.0011 0.0009
VC*RISK		0.0020 0.0026		0.0011 0.0010		0.0006 0.0007
TAX	0.3797 0.4103	-0.2523 0.2121	-0.0556 0.0436	-0.0218 0.0332	-0.0655 0.0883	-0.0596 0.0766
VC*TAX	-0.2542 0.4634	0.1836 0.2472	0.0066 0.0716	-0.0905 0.0571	-0.0466 0.1050	-0.0765 0.0875
NDTS	-1.6452 2.9555	-0.3141 0.7518	-0.0752 0.1137	-0.0639 0.0756	0.0747 0.2259	-0.2057 0.3334
VC*NDTS	1.7428 3.0359	0.1285 0.8416	-0.0170 0.1288	-0.0369 0.0858	-0.3467 0.2248	-0.0281 0.3239
VC		-1.8620 1.9009		0.1596 0.5447		-0.9682 0.7900
SH_VC		0.6064** 0.2971		0.0216 0.1879	-0.0079 0.4982	0.0647 0.1711
SH_INS		0.1141 0.1850		0.0372 0.0719	0.2652 0.1815	0.0883 0.0905
R² within	0.5856	0.1264	0.5076	0.4494	0.2106	0.1990
R² between	0.1522	0.2204	0.0524	0.4616	0.0031	0.2901
R² overall	0.0195	0.1899	0.1071	0.4584	0.0054	0.2262
F-test	4.4822***	1.1446	11.9390***	7.0098***	2.4082***	4.3958***
F-test (interactive terms)	0.5423	0.4972	1.0936	1.7052*	0.4935	2.1578***
Hausman test		293.9121***		na		na

The results of the F-tests are qualitatively identical to Table 6. With the exception of the random effects specification for the years preceding the IPO, all estimations turn out to be highly significant. In addition, the Hausman-test rejects the null hypothesis of relatively higher efficiency of the RE-specification pre-IPO. A remarkable insight comes from the combined significance test on the interactive VC terms. For the period after the IPO as well as for the estimation with all periods the values of the F-statistic suggest that the relationship between the debt ratio and main capital structure determinants, i.e. age, size, tangibility, liquidity, profitability, growth, risk and taxes is influenced by VC involvement.

Contrary to the estimates in the previous section without interactive terms, the coefficient of the variable AGE is now negative for the time after the IPO and for the regression on the sample including all years. This finding superficially contradicts our hypothesis. However, for the same periods the interactive term of age with VC involvement is significantly different from zero and has the opposite sign. This implies that after the IPO the debt ratio increases with age for VC financed companies while it decreases for all other companies ceteris paribus. The significance of the interactive term post-IPO is remarkable in the light of our expected, vanishing influence of ownership structure after a company has gone public. Company size measured by total assets exerts a negative impact on the debt ratio in the estimate including all years, which is again contrary to the theoretically derived relationship.

Compared to the estimates without interactive terms the variables for tangibility have lost significance. The coefficients of the relative level of inventory are consistent with our hypotheses only for the time after the IPO. We interpret the negative coefficient of the variable inventory and the positive sign of interactive term inventory with VC involvement for the years before the IPO as indicators of perceived management quality by banks. Usually, high inventories can be a signal of overestimated demand and consequently show management failures. However, the reputation of a VC investor can turn this interpretation into a necessary precondition for future growth. The positive coefficient of VC involvement and account receivable post-IPO points into the right direction, although it is not obvious why higher levels of accounts receivable should positively affect the debt ratio in VC financed companies and remain without effect in others. The results for the liquidity and profitability variables confirm the results of previous section's estimates. In particular, the lack of significance of the interactive terms suggests that companies with and without VC involvement do apparently not differ with respect to capital structure choice along these characteristics. In line with expected behavior, the growth rate of total assets exerts a negative influence on the debt ratio pre-IPO. However, the negative relationship post-IPO contradicts the hypothesis. The significant, positive coefficient of the corresponding, interactive term suggests that the relationship between growth rates and the debt ratio is different for VC financed companies. Finally, the positive coefficient of the relative equity share of VC investors, SH_VC, supports the hypothesis and the results of the previous section.

6 Conclusions

Existing empirical evidence on the relationship between VC financing and capital structure choice for growth companies is quite scarce and partly inconsistent. This study contributes to filling this gap by analyzing how the involvement of VC investors in the financing of growth companies affects capital structure choice.

The results of panel regressions for the time before and after the IPO show that the involvement of VC investors in the financing of growth companies significantly affects their capital structure choice. Specifically, VC involvement implies lower debt ratios, which supports the hypothesis that VC financed companies need to rely on debt to a lesser extent. Moreover, higher relative equity shares of VC investors are accompanied by higher debt ratios which in turn provide evidence for the profit-maximizing behavior of VC investors during the time before an IPO. After the going public, the null hypothesis of missing relevance of VC financing variables for the debt ratio can generally not be rejected. This is in line with the expected disappearance of VC investors' influence on financing decisions once ownership becomes widely dispersed.

Most other capital structure determinants behave in the predicted way (see Table 8). While higher tangibility is associated with higher debt ratios, higher liquidity, profitability and risk imply lower levels of debt. The evidence on company size however, is contrary to the hypothesis while the evidence on growth does not turn out to be consistent for the two items annual growth rate of total assets and of net revenues over all periods.

Table 8. VC impact on capital structure choice: Empirical results support hypotheses
The book value of debt divided by the book value of total assets is used as a measure of capital structure and as dependent variable in the regressions. The results for the independent variables in the regression are carried out for three different time frames: all years of the dataset, the time before the IPO and the time after the IPO. The symbols indicate ✓ congruence, n.s.: not significant, × contradiction and ? mixed results for the hypothesis and the empirical results, + positively related, - negatively related, O not significantly related.

	Pre-IPO			Post-IPO			Overall		
	Hyp.	Empir.	Congr.	Hypo.	Empir.	Congr.	Hypo.	Empir.	Congr.
Age	-	-		+	O	n.s.	O	-	×
Size	+	-	×	+	O	n.s.	+	-	×
Tangibility	+	O	n.s.	+	+		+	+	
Liquidity	-	O	n.s.	-	-		-	-	
Profitability	-	O	n.s.	-	-		-	-	
Growth	-	-		+	+		O	?	?
Risk	-	O	n.s.	-	-		-	O	n.s.
Taxes	O	O		O	-	×	O	O	
Tax-Shield	O	O		O	O		O	O	
VC-Financing	-	-		O	O		-		
VC-Share	+	+		O	O			O	
Insider-Share	+	O	n.s.	O	O			O	

Results according to Wenzel (2006), S. 364.

Table 9. VC vs. non-VC financed companies: Only scattered evidence with regard to VC interaction terms
The book value of debt divided by the book value of total assets is used as a measure of capital structure and as dependent variable in the regressions. The results for the independent variables and the VC interaction terms in the regression are carried out for three different time frames: all years of the dataset, the time before the IPO and the time after the IPO. The symbols indicate + = positively related, - = negatively related, o = not significantly related.

Capital structure determinants

	Pre-IPO	Post-IPO	Overall
Age	o	–	–
Size	o	o	–
Tangibility	–	+	o
Liquidity	o	–	–
Profitability	o	–	o
Growth	–	–	o
Risk	o	o	o
Taxes	o	o	o
Tax-Shield	o	o	o
VC-Financing	o	o	o
VC-Share	+	o	o
Insider-Share	o	o	o

Interaction terms with VC-financing

	Pre-IPO	Post-IPO	Overall
VC*Age	o	+	+
VC*Size	o	o	+
VC*Tangibility	+	+	o
VC*Liquidity	o	o	o
VC*Profitability	o	o	o
VC*Growth	+	+	o
VC*Risk	o	o	o
VC*Taxes	o	o	o
VC*Tax-Shield	o	o	o

While the evidence concerning the direct effect of VC involvement on capital structure choice is very strong, the results regarding the implications of VC financing on the relationship between other capital structure determinants and the debt ratio are not as clear. While we could not reject the null hypothesis of lacking impact of all interactive regressors combined, the results regarding the individual variables are scattered and in summary not conclusive (see Table 9). However, it appears that the relationship between the debt ratio and company age, size and growth are different between companies financed with venture capital and those without.

By providing evidence for the strong link between VC involvement in the financing of growth companies we have highlighted the importance of ownership structure especially for companies with concentrated groups of investors. While the results are strong for the direct impact of VC financing on capital structure choice, the indirect effects certainly warrant further investigation. This will be a task for future research.

References

Admati A, Pfleiderer A (1994) Robust Financial Contracting and the Role of Venture Capitalists. Journal of Finance 49:371–402

Anderson RW, Nyborg KG (2001) Financing and Corporate Growth under Repeated Moral Hazard, Financial Markets Group, London School of Economics and Political Science. Discussion Paper No. 376

Audretsch DB, Lehmann EE (2003) Debt or Equity? The Role of Venture Capital in Financing the New Economy in Germany. CEPR Discussion Paper No. 3656
Autore D, Kovacs T (2004) The Pecking Order Theory and Time-Varying Adverse Selection Costs. Department of Finance, Pamplin College of Business, Virginia
Baltagi BH (1996) Econometric Analysis of Panel Data. John Wiley & Sons, Chicester 1996
Bascha A, Walz U (2001) Convertible Securities and Optimal Exit Decisions in Venture Capital Finance. Journal of Corporate Finance 7:285–306
Baxter ND (1967) Leverage, Risk of Ruin and the Cost of Capital. Journal of Finance 22:395–403
Börner CJ, Grichnik D, Reize F (2009) Finanzierungsentscheidungen mittelständischer Unternehmer – Einflussfaktoren der Fremdfinanzierung deutscher KMU. Zeitschrift für betriebswirtschaftliche Forschung, in press
Berger AN, Udell GF (1998) The Economics of Small Business Finance: The Roles of Private Equity and Debt Markets in the Financial Growth Cycle. Journal of Banking and Finance 22:613–673
Bessler W, Kurth A (2004) Finanzierungsstrukturen von Neuemissionen. Finanz Betrieb 6:59–69
Brav A, Gompers PA (1997) Myth or Reality? The Long-Run Underperformance of Initial Public Offerings: Evidence form Venture and Nonventure Capital-Backed Companies. Journal of Finance 52:1791–1821
Cassar G (2001) The Financing and Capital Structure of Business Start-Ups: The Importance of Asset Structure. Frontiers of Entrepreneurship Research
Cassar G, Holmes S (2003) Capital structure and financing of SMEs: Australian evidence. Accounting & Finance 43:123–147
Castanias R (1983) Bankruptcy Risk and Optimal Capital Structure. Journal of Finance 38:1617–1635
Chittenden F, Hall G, Hutchinson P (1996) Small Firm Growth, Access to Capital Markets and Financial Structure: Review of Issues and Empirical Investigation. Small Business Economics 8:59–67
Churchill N, Lewis V (1983) The Five Stages of Small Business Growth. Harvard Business Review (May-June), 30-39
Cornell B, Shapiro AC (1988) Financing Corporate Growth. Journal of Applied Corporate Finance 1:6–22
DeAngelo H, Masulis RW (1980) Optimal Capital Structure Under Corporate and Personal Taxation. Journal of Financial Economics 8:3–30
Denis DJ (2004) Entrepreneurial Finance: An Overview of the Issues and Evidence. Journal of Corporate Finance 10:301–326
Dewatripont M, Legros P, Matthews SA (2002) Moral Hazard and Capital Structure Dynamics, PIER Working Paper, Penn Institute for Economic Research, University of Pennsylvania
Fischer EO, Heinkel R, Zechner J (1989) Dynamic Capital Structure Choice: Theory and Tests. Journal of Finance 44:19–40
Frank MZ, Goyal VK (2003) Capital Structure Decisions, Faculty of Commerce, University of British Columbia. Working Paper
Garmaise M (1997) Informed Investors and the Financing of Entrepreneurial Projects. Stanford University, Working Paper
Gompers PA (1995) Optimal Investment. Monitoring and the Staging of Venture Capital. Journal of Finance 50:1461–1489
Gompers PA (1999) Ownership and Control in Entrepreneurial Firms: An Examination of Convertible Securities in Venture Capital Investments, Harvard Business School, Boston. Working Paper
Hall G, Hutchinson P, Michaelas N (2004) Determinants of the Capital Structures of European SMEs. Journal of Business Finance & Accounting 31:711–728
Hanks SH et al (1993) Tightening the Life-Cycle Construct: A Taxonomic Study of Growth Change Configurations in High-Technology Organizations. Entrepreneurship Theory and Practice 17:5–29
Harris M, Raviv A (1991) The Theory of Capital Structure. Journal of Finance 46:297–355
Hausman JA (1978) Specification Tests in Econometrics. Econometrica 46:1251–1271
Helwege J, Liang N (1996) Is There a Pecking Order? Evidence from a Panel of IPO Firms. Journal of Financial Economics 40:429–458
Heymann D, DeLoof M, Ooghe H (2008) The Financial Structure of Private Held Belgian Firms. Small Business Economics 31:301–313
Hirshleifer D (1970) Investment, Interest and Capital, Prentice Hall, Englewood Cliffs, NJ 1970
Huyghebaert N, Van de Gucht LM (2002) The Determinants of Financial Structure: New Insights from Business Start-Ups, Department of Applied Economics (DETW). Katholieke Universiteit Leuven, 2002
Jensen MC, Meckling W (1976) Theory of the Firm: Managerial Behavior, Agency Costs and Capital Structure. Journal of Financial Economics 3:305–360

Kim EH (1978) A Mean-Variance Theory of Optimal Capital Structure and Corporate Debt Capacity. Journal of Finance 33:45–63
Kraus A, Litzenberger RH (1973) A State-Preference Model of Optimal Financial Leverage. Journal of Finance 28:911–922
Lerner J (1995) Venture Capitalists and the Oversight of Private Firms. Journal of Finance 50:301–318
López-Gracia J, Sogorb-Mira F (2008) Testing Trade-Off and Pecking Order Theories Financing SMEs. Small Business Economics 31:117–136
Masulis RW, Nahata R (2008) Venture Capital Conflicts of Interest: Evidence from Acquisitions of Venture Backed Firms, European Corporate Governance Institute. Finance Working Paper, No. 211
Michaelas N, Chittenden F, Poutziouris P (1999) Financial Policy and Capital Structure Choice in U.K. SMEs: Empirical Evidence from Company Panel Data. Small Business Economics 22:113–130
Modigliani F, Miller MH (1963) Corporate Income Taxes and the Cost of Capital: A Correction, American Economic Review 53:433–443
Myers SC (1977) Determinants of Corporate Borrowing. Journal of Financial Economics 5:147–175
Myers SC (1984) The Capital Structure Puzzle. Journal of Finance 39:575–592
Myers SC, Majluf NS (1984) Corporate Financing and Investment Decisions when Firms Have Information that Investors Do Not Have. Journal of Financial Economics 13:187–221
Rajan RG, Zingales L (1995) What Do We Know About Capital Structure? Some Evidence from International Data. Journal of Finance 50:1421–1460
Robichek AA, Myers SC (1966) Problems in the Theory of Optimal Capital Structure. Journal of Financial and Quantitative Analysis 1:1–35
Sahlman WA (1990) The Structure and Governance of Venture Capital Organizations. Journal of Financial Economics 27:473–521
Sánchez-Vidal J, Martín-Ugedo J (2005) Financing Preferences of Spanish Firms: Evidence on the Pecking Order Theory. Review of Quantitative Finance & Accounting 25:341–355
Smith CW Jr, Wakeman L (1985) Determinants of Corporate Leasing Policy. Journal of Finance 40:895–908
Smith CW Jr, Warner JB (1979) On Financial Contracting: An Analysis of Bond Covenants. Journal of Financial Economics 7:117–161
Sogorb-Mira F (2005) How SME Uniqueness Affects Capital Structure: Evidence From A 1994–1998 Spanish Data Panel. Small Business Economics 25:447–457
Titman S, Wessels R (1988) The Determinants of Capital Structure Choice. Journal of Finance 43:1–19
Tykvová T (2003) The Decision of Venture Capitalists on Timing and Extent of IPOs, Centre of European Economic Research (ZEW). Discussion Paper
Voulgaris F, Asteriou D, Agiomirgianakis G (2004) Size and Determinants of Capital Structure in the Greek Manufacturing Sector. International Review of Applied Economics 2:247–262
Walker D (1989) Financing the Small Firm. Small Business Economics 1:285–296
Wenzel A (2006) Kapitalstrukturpolitik in Wachstumsunternehmen. Eine empirische Untersuchung deutscher Unternehmen auf Basis von Jahresabschlussinformationen, Bad Soden/Ts.
White H (1984) Asymptotic Theory for Econometricians. Academic Press, Orlando, FL
Zoppa A, McMahon RGP (2002) Pecking Order Theory and the Financial Structure of Manufacturing SMEs from Australia´s Business Longitudinal Survey, School of Commerce. Research Paper Series, No. 1

Strategisches IP-Management – Der Weg zum Monopol ↗

WWW.GABLER.I

Mittelstaedt, Axel
Strategisches IP-Management – mehr als nur Patente
Geistiges Eigentum schützen und als Wettbewerbsvorsprung nutzen
2009. 259 S. Mit 38 Abb. u. 3 Tab.
Br. EUR 69,00
ISBN 978-3-8349-1399-9

Axel Mittelstaedt zeigt in diesem Buch erstmalig, wie es gelingt, Namen, technische Spezifikationen oder gestalterische Besonderheiten mithilfe von Schutzrechten auch auf internationalem Terrain erfolgreich zu verteidigen, um so Produktpiraterie und Preisdumping entgegenzuwirken. An zahlreichen Beispielen wird deutlich, wie das gesamte geistige Eigentum eines Unternehmens mit Marketing und Unternehmenskommunikation vernetzt werden kann, um eine Monopolstellung zu erreichen. Ein gewinnbringendes Buch gerade für Nicht-Juristen wie Führungsverantwortliche in mittelständischen und größeren Unternehmen, Marketingmanager und Leiter Unternehmenskommunikation.

Der Inhalt
- Vorsprung schaffen durch Strategisches Intellectual Property Management
- Die Bedeutung des SIP für die Markenstrategie
- Schutzrechtspositionen aufbauen
- Ideen und Design systematisch schützen
- SIP und integrierte Unternehmenskommunikation
- Fragenkatalog SIP für Entscheider

Die Autoren
Axel Mittelstaedt ist Rechtsanwalt für Marken-, Wettbewerbs-, Geschmacksmuster- und Patentrecht und seit 25 Jahren im gewerblichen Rechtsschutz tätig. Er ist Mitglied des Vorstands des Marketing-Clubs Köln/Bonn und gefragter Referent.

Einfach bestellen:
kerstin.kuchta@gwv-fachverlage.de
Telefon +49(0)611. 7878-626

KOMPETENZ IN SACHEN WIRTSCHAFT

Linking Incorporated Cultural and Financial Capital of the Entrepreneur in a New Venture Creation Context: A Cross-Country Comparison

Malgorzata A. Wdowiak, Erich J. Schwarz, Robert J. Breitenecker, Rainer Harms

Abstract: New venture creation is usually focused around the founder who has to accumulate the resources needed to run the venture. Financial resources are one of the most crucial resources in this context. Taking into account the importance of the founder for the acquisition of financial capital, we argue that the cultural capital theory could advance entrepreneurship research by extending the discussion to cultural investments. The issue of culturally bounded behavior of the founder reveals an important research gap. According to the theory of cultural capital, cultural habits (expressed by values), knowledge and skills developed in the process of cultural socialization and work experience are crucial to behavior and outcomes in the context of social actions performed by the individual. Based on that theory, we explore the effects of individualistic and collectivistic values, knowledge acquired through work experience, and entrepreneurial skills on the amount of initial financial capital. We test the model in two countries with different cultural environments and at different stages of economic development: in Austria (n=127), which has a longer individualistic tradition, and in Poland (n=136) with its communist, collectivistic legacy. We found that collectivistic values, entrepreneurial skills, and industry experience have a significant impact on the amount of initial financial capital in both countries. In the comparative country context, especially the relationship between industry experience of Austrian founders and the amount of initial financial capital proved to be stronger than that of their Polish counterparts.

Keywords: New venture creation · Initial financial capital · Cultural capital · Collectivistic values · Individualistic values

JEL Classification: L26 · D24 · Z13

Dipl.-Kff. Mag. M. A. Wdowiak (✉)
Klagenfurt University, Department of Innovation Management and Entrepreneurship, Universitaetsstrasse 65–67, 9020 Klagenfurt, Austria, Tel.: 0043-463-2700-4059, E-mail: malgorzata.wdowiak@uni-klu.ac.at

Univ.-Prof. Dr. E. J. Schwarz (✉)
Klagenfurt University, Department of Innovation Management and Entrepreneurship, Universitaetsstrasse 65–67, 9020 Klagenfurt, Austria, Tel.: 0043-463-2700-4051, E-mail: erich.schwarz@uni-klu.ac.at

Dr. R. J. Breitenecker (✉)
Klagenfurt University, Department of Innovation Management and Entrepreneurship, Universitaetsstrasse 65–67, 9020 Klagenfurt, Austria, Tel.: 0043-463-2700-4053, E-mail: robert.breitenecker@uni-klu.ac.at

PD Dr. R. Harms (✉)
University of Twente – NIKOS, Dutch Institute for Knowledge Intensive Entrepreneurship, Capitool 15, Room C-305, 7500 AE Enschede, The Netherlands, Tel. 0031-53-489-3907, E-mail: r.harms@utwente.nl

1 Introduction

New ventures are a critical component of the development of free-market economies (Smallbone and Welter, 2001; Lyles et al., 2004). Even though new ventures start with an idea in the mind of the founder, in the later stage of the venture creation process, financial resources are needed. A solid financial capital basis creates a cushion against random shocks and supports the venture's ability to undertake corrective actions, and it facilitates investments in product/service development, production, and marketing (Chandler and Hanks, 1998). Pertaining to the amount of finance needed for startup, a special report on financing by the Global Entrepreneurship Monitor (Bygrave and Hunt, 2005) reveals that the average amount needed to start a business is 53,673 US$. On average, the founders themselves provide 65.8 percent of the start-up capital for their new ventures. To meet the financing needs of new venture creation and early growth, a founder often needs to tap external capital sources (Bates, 1990) such as banks (debt capital) or business angels and venture capital companies (equity capital).

However, (additional) financial capital may be difficult to obtain. For example, new ventures may not have a track record of a successful business history, and founders may have little collateral. This makes capital suppliers reluctant to provide funds. Previous research on the acquisition of finance that incorporates the role of the founder tended to deal with the impact of selected investments in human capital, such as education or job training (Hsu, 2007; Blumberg and Letterie, 2008). The literature suggests that factors such as gender (Cassar, 2004) and previous work experience (Kim, 2006) may affect the ability of the founder to acquire additional funds.

However, most studies have neglected the *cultural background* of the entrepreneur. This is surprising, because as already as at the beginning of 20th century, Max Weber (1930) viewed economic outcomes as the product of cultural values built around the Protestant ideals. Only a few conceptual works dealt with the role of cultural values in an entrepreneurship context. For example, Tiessen (1997) argues that individualism may be vital in generating the variety of organizational resources. Taking into account the importance of the founder for the acquisition of financial capital, we argue that the cultural capital theory could advance entrepreneurship research by extending the discussion to the founder's cultural investments. According to the theory of cultural capital, habits (expressed by values), knowledge and skills developed in the process of cultural socialization and work experience are fundamental to behavior and outcomes in the context of social activities performed by the individual. These personal characteristics constitute incorporated cultural capital. We propose that the inclusion of incorporated cultural capital has the potential to go beyond the explicatory power of human capital in the analysis of new venture creation.

Given that the cultural background of the entrepreneur is important, it is noteworthy that previous research tended to focus on *established market economies* such as the United States and Western Europe, areas with abundant resources, entrepreneurial role models and stable, institutional environments. The situation of entrepreneurs creating their ventures in *emerging economies* with scarce resources, unstable institutions and a limited entrepreneurship tradition remains under-researched (Bruton and Ahlstrom, 2005).

The above problem outline results in two research questions:

- What personal factors do influence initial financial capital?
- Do those effects depend on the country context (emerging vs. mature economies)?

Our research addresses two issues. First, we explore the effects of individualistic and collectivistic cultural values, knowledge and entrepreneurial skills on the amount of initial financial capital used for founding. Thereby individualistic values relate to self-reliance, competition, social status, and enjoyment, and collectivistic values pertain to group orientation, stability of relationships, equality, safety, and harmony (Green ct al., 2005; Morris and Schindehutte, 2005). Second, we examine whether the same factors affect the amount of initial financial capital in the same way in both emerging and mature economies.

We test the model in two countries with different cultural environments and at different stages of economic development: in Austria, which has a longer individualistic tradition, and in Poland with its communist, collectivistic legacy. Austria with a Gross Domestic Product per capita of 36,980 US$ in 2005 (World Bank, 2006) represents mature economies with rich financial resources, developed capital markets, and stable institutional environment. Poland with a GDP per capita of 7,943.34 US$ in 2005 represents medium advanced transition economies. The research is based on a survey conducted in 2007 among new ventures that were created six months prior to data collection (Austria: n=127, Poland: n=136). To test the hypotheses, we apply a hierarchical multiple linear regression model and a proportional-odds model. The interaction effects with the country dummy are included to test for significant country differences. Because initial financial capital depends to a high degree on industry, we control the model for industries.

The remainder of the paper is structured as follows. First, we provide a theoretical background with an emphasis on cultural capital theory. In Section 3, we discuss the results of previous research on the role of the founder's cultural capital in the financing of a new venture. In Section 4, hypotheses linking cultural capital and initial financial capital as well as country differences are proposed. In Section 5, the sample and the methods used are presented. In the subsequent part (Section 6), the results are reported and discussed. Finally, we provide conclusions and suggest implications for future research.

2 Cultural and Financial Capital of the Entrepreneur: Theoretical Background

2.1 Traditional and Contemporary Concepts of Capital

An early understanding of the concept of capital encompassed financial capital in terms of circulating capital to embody stock in trade and work in progress (Table 1). Capital was understood as complementary to labor in its role to catalyze and to facilitate the creation of surplus (Kregel, 1976). Taking another perspective, Ricardo viewed capital and labor as substitutes rather than complementary assets (Ricardo, 1895). Other classical economists attempted to categorize capital as stored up labor: "... besides the primary and universal requisites of production... there is another... namely, a stock, previously accumulated, of the products of former labor – this accumulation stock is termed capital. The distinction, then, between capital and not-capital does not lie in the kind of commodities, but in the mind of the capitalist – in his will to employ them for one purpose rather than another" (John Stuart Mill quoted in: Fisher, 1896, p. 511). Neoclassical economists treated capital and labor as equally important factors of production. In addition to that, they conceptualized capital as homogeneous, interchangeable units. So, capital can occur in monetary form and can be expressed in monetary terms (Dean and Kretschmer, 2007; Kregel, 1976; Fisher, 1896).

While traditional concepts of capital focused on financial and physical capital as factors of production, contemporary, *postindustrial* concepts also view as capital other factors that have the capacity to produce economically desirable outcomes. In the 1960s, the capital metaphor was extended to *human capital* arising from the realization that knowledge, know-how and expertise residing in the individual constitute a capital stock that can be utilized to produce economic outputs (Mincer, 1958; Schultz, 1961; Becker, 1962). Such capital is also the result of past effort (Becker, 1962). In the 1980s, the concept of *social capital* emerged viewing social capital as the "aggregate of the actual or potential resources which are linked to possession of a durable network of more or less institutionalized relationships of mutual acquaintance and recognition" (Bourdieu, 1986, p. 248). A central premise of that approach is that social embeddedness of the individual may be regarded as a channel to relevant resources and thus as catalyst to value creation (Coleman, 1988). Also in the 1980s, the concept of *cultural capital* was developed to ac-

Table 1. Conceptualizations of Capital

Author(s) of the Concept	Characteristics	Function
Smith	In monetary form; circulating capital; linked to economic actor – capitalist	To facilitate production; complementary to labor in production process, but not by itself a source of surplus
Ricardo	Circulating capital; not only in monetary form, but also as physical capital (e.g. machinery); measurable; ownership clear	To account for industrial capital viewed as part of wealth creation; substitutable for labor
Mill; Marx	Product of past labor; tangible; linked to economic actor	To supply current productive labor
Neoclassical economists	Investment employed; financial and physical capital valued in monetary form; tangible	To enable the return on capital and wages to be viewed as equivalents; to enable output of past to contribute to current production
Mincer; Schultz; Becker	In form of knowledge and expertise; product of past labor; embodied in the individual; intangible; less measurable	To account for the return on investments in the form of intangibles such as education and work experience
Coleman; Bourdieu	In form of networks and resources that can be accessed through those networks; embodied in relationships with others; difficult to measure	To account for the value added from utilization of capacities that reside outside the economic actor
Bourdieu	In forms of institutionalized assets such as education diplomas and incorporated ones such as knowledge, abilities, and cultural values	To account for the return on cultural investments

Sources: Dean and Kretschmer (2007); Coleman (1988); Bourdieu (1986); Becker (1962)

count for the return on cultural investments such as cultural values in social processes (Bourdieu, 1986). Bourdieu's concept of cultural capital came out initially from his research on inequalities in scholastic achievement that dealt with the effects of family background and cultural transmission (Bourdieu and Passeron, 1977).

New forms of capital differ from traditional concepts in many respects. They are usually intangible, difficult to measure, embodied in economic actors or in relationships between them. In contemporary concepts, capital is not necessarily static as in traditional economic concepts and includes dynamic components as processes (e.g. social (relational) capital). Those new concepts also share some similarities with traditional approaches, e.g. capital is still a product of past labor[1]. But adopting the capital metaphor to the contemporary concepts primarily lies in their *explanatory role*. They are classified as capital because they facilitate or determine the value creation process, as well as enabling the distinction of other factors of production (Dean and Kretschmer, 2007; Swartz, 1997). New capital categories allow to capture less measurable aspects of the value creation process that explain differences in outcomes in apparently identical production processes (Dean and Kretschmer, 2007; Robinson et al., 2002). Concepts of human and social capital have already been recognized in entrepreneurship research (Witt, 2004; Davidsson and Honig, 2003; Brüderl and Preisendörfer, 1998; Cooper et al., 1994; Aldrich and Zimmer, 1986). But the analysis of cultural capital has not been given much attention in entrepreneurship literature (Firkin, 2001).

In the following discussion, we turn our attention to the concept of cultural capital. For culture to be a useful explanatory construct in the entrepreneurial context, we must first unveil its identity. So, before discussing the relationship of cultural and financial capital of the economic actor, we consider what culture means and in what way culture can be interpreted as capital.

2.2 Conceptualizing Cultural Capital and the Theory of Cultural Capital

In contemporary concepts of culture, attention is given to implicit and explicit patterns of meanings, practices, and artifacts distributed throughout the context in which an individual participates, and how these guide individuals' behavior (Markus and Hamedani, 2007). We define culture as "causally distributed patterns of mental representations, their public expression, and the resultant behaviors in given (…) contexts" (Atran et al., 2005, p. 751). Culture can be characterized by three essential aspects (Triandis, 2007). First, culture emerges in adoptive interaction between individuals and social environments. Second, culture consists of shared elements (values and practices). Third, culture is transmitted across time periods and generations.

Adopting the capital metaphor to culture, we focus on its *value* to the economic actors. There are two essential functions of culture that allow us to view it as a stock of values that may give rise to economic outcomes (Triandis, 2007; Throsby, 1999). First, culture enables the individual to understand his or her relationship with the environment and to predict events (knowledge function). Second, as a result of interaction with the environment, culture provides norms that furnish guidance for behavior and maximize the chances to receive desirable rewards and minimize costs (adjustment function). Similar to capital theorists who view capital as stored up effort, culture may be conceptualized as the *"knowledge stored up* (in memories of men, in books and objects) for future use – patterns for doing certain things in certain ways" (Kluckhohn, 1962, p. 25).

As early as in the first half of the Twentieth century, sociologist Max Weber (1930) acknowledged that both cultural and economic resources shape a society's power structures. In Weber's theory of status groups, culture is vital to social order and thus to capitalism. Building on cultural ideas of Weber and Durkheim,[2] Bourdieu (1986) conceptualized cultural capital as another principle of stratification, turning the attention of scholars to *symbolic and economic power* of culture in social processes (Farkas, 1996).[3]

Bourdieu distinguishes between the *objectified cultural capital* that refers to material objects of cultural value an individual possesses such as artworks or books (Table 2), the individual's *institutionalized cultural capital* such as education diplomas, academic degrees and occupational certificates, and the individual's *incorporated cultural capital* such as knowledge, skills and habits in form of long-lasting dispositions of the mind such as cultural values (Bourdieu, 1986, p. 243-248). The two latter forms of cultural capital exhibit a dualism with regard to knowledge and skills (Lareau and Weininger, 2004). Institutionalized cultural capital is conceptualized as a more objective form of the incorporated cultural capital (Bourdieu, 1986, p. 246). Certificates and diplomas legitimate acquired academic degrees and work achievements, thus indirectly validating the knowledge and skills an individual holds. They constitute the foundation for access possibilities to occupy a specific work position (e.g. director in public administration) and to perform a specific profession (e.g. a university professor). Incorporated cultural capital directly refers to acquired knowledge and skills that are memorized and internalized in the person.[4]

In Bourdieurian theory of cultural capital, knowledge, skills and habits that are embodied in the person are *most crucial* to behavior and outcomes in the context of social actions performed by the individual (Bourdieu, 1986, p. 244). Taking into account the importance of the founder for the acquisition of financial capital, we draw attention to the incorporated cultural capital of the founder in the subsequent discussion.

Incorporated cultural capital appears to share some similarities with human capital components (e.g. Becker, 1993).[5] Thus, it is vital to understand where the boundaries between human and cultural capital theories lie. A most essential distinction between cultural and human capital theories refers to different premises. Contrary to human capital representatives, Bourdieu does not share the assumption of a rational-actor approach. Becker (1993, p. 17) states that investments in human capital "usually are rational responses to a calculus of expected costs and benefits". Bourdieu (1986) argues that the

Table 2. Forms of Cultural Capital

Cultural Capital	Characteristics
objectified cultural capital	material objects of cultural value such as books, works of art, instruments or machines
institutionalized cultural capital	education diplomas, academic degrees, occupational certificates
incorporated cultural capital	knowledge, skills and habits in form of long-lasting dispositions of the mind such as cultural values or language

Source: Bourdieu (1986)

choices and actions of individuals are patterned and interest-oriented at a *tacit, pre-reflective* level of awareness. They reflect both the accumulated capital from the *past life and work experience* of the individual and the present opportunities and constraints of the field in which they act. The accumulation of cultural capital in its embodied form begins at a young age by "pedagogical actions" occurring in families and schools (Swartz, 1997, p. 76). These actions may pass unnoticed at that time, but they constitute the central mechanisms by which individual outcomes are determined. The *cultural socialization* is what provides the individuals with assets such as norms, cultural values or language, which are necessary for acting and participating within their society (Clausen, 1968).

Furthermore, Bourdieu criticizes proponents of human capital theories, stating that their discourse of individual productivity is usually reduced to "monetary investments and profits, or those [investments] directly convertible into money, such as the costs of schooling and the cash equivalent of time devoted to study" (Bourdieu, 1986, p. 243). Subtle dimensions of cultural socialization, which usually cannot be easily quantified in monetary terms, are disregarded in human capital theories. Thus, important cultural investments prior to transition into adulthood remain neglected: "They [human capital theoreticians] inevitably, by a necessary paradox, let slip the best hidden and socially most determinant educational investment, namely the domestic transition of cultural capital" (Bourdieu, 1986, p. 244).[6] An additional difference between human and cultural capital may lie in the origin of capital. Both forms of capital are embodied in the economic actor, but cultural capital is partly accumulated through the (unconscious) transfer of cultural assets from one to the next generation within a family and may therefore be considered to a certain degree *family-embedded* and *collectively-inherited*. On the other hand, accumulation of human capital mostly occurs as a result of idiosyncratic, calculated (conscious) investments (Robinson et al., 2002).

In theory of cultural capital, Bourdieu (1986) emphasizes that various forms of cultural capital can be interchangeable. In the context of incorporated cultural capital, he stresses that "ability [skill] or talent is itself the product of an investment of time and cultural capital" (Bourdieu, 1986, p. 244)[7], where cultural capital pertains in this respect to long-standing dispositions of mind such as values, but also to the acquired and memorized knowledge (Lareau and Weininger, 2004; Bourdieu, 1986). We consider the stated interdependences between skills and other dimensions of cultural value in the subsequent analysis.

Over the past decade, a few management scholars have attempted to implement Bourdieu's approach in the business sciences, recognizing the need to extend the logic of economic analysis to apparently non-economic goods such as culture (Bowman, 2007; Ndofor and Priem, 2005). Though the effects of incorporated cultural capital conceptualized by Bourdieu remain under-researched in the context of venture financing to date, distinct dimensions of that capital have been already discussed in diverse financing contexts. The following section presents the main results of previous research.

3 Cultural and Financial Capital in the Context of New Venture Creation: Previous Research

In the previous literature, some factors related to founders' personal characteristics that may explain the amount of initial financial capital have already been discussed (e.g. Marlow and Patton, 2006; Cassar, 2004). A literature analysis of new venture finance in the five leading entrepreneurship journals[8] between 2004 and 2008 discovered 19 studies that deal with the effects of founders' profile and behavior. Studies that were based on small and medium enterprises and studies that apply to a later stage in the financial growth cycle, for example those that focus on venture capital, are not included.

In Table 3, the results of this literature analysis are given. In chronological order, studies on new venture finance are listed with a focus on the degree to which aspects of the founder such as knowledge gained through experience (industry, leadership, founding), entrepreneurial skills, habits (e.g. cultural values) and other person-related factors such as gender impact aspects of new venture financing.

With respect to incorporated cultural capital, knowledge acquired through work experience has been extensively covered in previous research on new venture finance (e.g. Blumberg and Letterie, 2008; Cassar, 2004). Higher investments in experience are especially supportive for obtaining loans or searching for external investors due to lowering the risk of investments (Bruns et al., 2008; Cassar, 2004). In contrast, entrepreneurial abilities have only been discussed in a small number of studies (e.g. Colombo and Grilli, 2007) and primarily in a debt capital context. Entrepreneurial skills are treated as investments that facilitate financing of new ventures and secure future rewards. Cultural dispositions of entrepreneurs have not yet been examined in a startup financing context. The exception constitutes a study by Kim et al. (2006) who investigate the importance of cultural capital for entrepreneurial entry. However, it has to be noted that they concentrate their analysis merely on the effects of the occupational background of the founder's parents without explicitly considering cultural values.

The literature review shows that the majority of research addressing the effects of factors related to the person upon financing new ventures intends to explain gender differences due to expected behavioral disparities (Wu et al., 2007; Marlow and Patton, 2006). Women are more likely to be risk averse and to possess less capital due to, for example, wage differences on the labor market. That characteristic of female founders may be conceived as barrier by new venture capitalization.

The analysis also demonstrates that the majority of studies are set in the context of traditional market economies. Exceptions are Hutchinson and Xavier (2006) who compare ventures from a mature market economy (Belgium) with ventures from an advanced transition country (Slovenia). Also, Zhang et al. (2008) and Zhang and Wong (2008) compare ventures from a market economy (Singapore) with ventures from a non-market economy (China). While the findings of these authors highlight that the economic context does make a difference in terms of new venture finance, this perspective is not addressed explicitly in most studies.

To sum up, the analysis shows that the consideration of the impact of personal characteristics of the founder on his or her funding decision is an emerging field. Based on the importance that can be ascribed to components of cultural capital in the new venture development process, these factors ought not to be neglected in future research.

Table 3. Cultural Capital and Financing of a New Venture – Literature Review

Study	Sample	Entrepreneur Knowledge*	Skills	Habits**	Other var.***	Focus of the analysis
Cassar (2004)	292 startups	√		growth orientation	gender	Capital structure
Alsos et al. (2006)	360 founders			control aversion	gender	Actually obtained amounts of funding
Hanley and Girma (2006)	466 loan applications	√				Loan application success
Hutchinson and Xavier (2006)	4,248 micro firms	No information on the entrepreneur ****				The impact of finance constraints on growth
Kim (2006)	3,567 small firms	√			gender	Credit rationing, e.g. loan application success
Kim et al. (2006)	PSED data	√	√		education, entrepreneurial parents	Relative importance of human, cultural and financial capital on entrepreneurial entry
Marlow and Patton (2005)	meta analysis				gender	The disadvantage of women entrepreneurs in terms of accessing finance
Ou and Haynes (2006)	8,100 small firms				gender, minority	Internal equity use
Pindado et al. (2006)	402 small firms	No information on the entrepreneur ****				Debt ratios
Carter et al. (2007)	35 loan officers	√		commitment	education, marital status	Decision criteria used by male of female loan officers
Colombo and Grilli (2007)	386 startups	√	√			Access to bank loans
Freel (2007)	256 startups	No information on the entrepreneur ****				Loan application success
Huyghebaert et al. (2007)	325 startups	No information on the entrepreneur ****				Ratio of bank debt to trade credit debt
Blumberg and Letterie (2008)	1,140 potential starter	√	√		family, age, foreign origin	Acceptance or rejection of credit application
Bruns et al. (2008)	114 loan officers	√	√		similarity	Loan officer's decision policies
Heyman et al. (2008)	1,132 small firms	No information on the entrepreneur ****				Capital structure
Wu et al. (2007)	2,216 small family firms				gender, education, minority	The effect of family management on the use of equity
Zhang et al. (2008)	226 startups	√	√			Propensity to use networks to approach investors
Zhang and Wong (2008)	378 entrepreneurs	√			education	Propensity to use networks to approach investors

* knowledge gained through work experience; ** e.g. cultural values; *** e.g. gender, age, education;
**** the article deals only implicitly with the role of entrepreneur's profile in the given finance context

4 Effects of Cultural Capital of the Founder on Financial Capital: The Hypotheses

As Bourdieu (1986) states, knowledge, skills and cultural values – all constituting incorporated cultural capital of the economic actor – are crucial to the behavior and its results of individuals. In our research, we investigate how that cultural capital may be instrumental in increasing the founder's financial capital. Specifically, we examine the effects of entrepreneurial skills, individualistic values, collectivistic values, and knowledge accumulated through work experience on the amount of initial financial capital.

4.1 The Effects of Entrepreneurial Skills

Entrepreneurial skills are among the crucial components of cultural capital. They may be conceived as abilities to recognize and take advantage of a business opportunity (Chandler and Jansen, 1992; Chandler and Hanks, 1994). A key function of entrepreneurial skills is to acquire the resources needed to establish and to grow the venture. For example, given the scarcity of financial resources, an entrepreneur with superior entrepreneurial skills will be better able to access financial resources, either by bootstrapping or by convincing loan officers of the advantages of his/her credit application. This would in turn result in a greater availability of financial capital. A second line of argument that connects entrepreneurial skills with the amount of initial financial capital is based on the idea that founders well-equipped with entrepreneurial skills are able to conceive of more promising ventures. To the degree that these ventures may be more capital intensive than imitative ventures, and to the degree that founders who perceive that their ventures are more promising in terms of growth are likely to invest more of their own financial resources (Carter and Van Auken, 1990), we expect that these ventures will be provided with a higher amount of initial financial capital.

Pertaining to differences of the impact of entrepreneurial skills in different cultural contexts, we argue that the founder's ability to recognize and exploit new business opportunities is more crucial to the entrepreneurial process in less stable environments that lack abundant resources. According to Orazem and Vodopivec (1997, p. 896): "Disequilibrium and uncertainty create an increased need for entrepreneurial skills". Compared to mature economies, the institutional environment in transition economies is less developed and the market environment has less resources. This characterizes the context of a transition country as more turbulent and uncertain, so that entrepreneurial skills may be more relevant in acquiring initial financial capital in such hostile environment. Therefore, we hypothesize that:

Hypothesis 1a: *There will be a positive correlation between the entrepreneurial skills of the founder and initial financial capital.*
Hypothesis 1b: *The relationship between the entrepreneurial skills of founders and initial financial capital in a transition economy will be stronger than that of their counterparts in a mature economy.*

4.2 The Effects of Cultural Values

Cultural values are the next central element of incorporated cultural capital as they function to provide guidance in life (Kilby, 1993). While "entrepreneurial skills" is an acknowledged term in the entrepreneurship literature (Kennedy and Drennan, 2001), the meaning of cultural values is rather unknown. Therefore, we open the discussion with relevant insights from cultural sciences.

Schwartz (1992, p. 4) defines values as "concepts or beliefs that pertain to desirable end states or behaviors and transcend specific situations in guiding selection or evaluation of behavior and events and are ordered by relative importance". In previous studies on cultural influence, individualism and collectivism are the most researched dimensions of culture (Chiu and Hong, 2006). They are usually conceptualized as opposite characteristics (e.g. Hofstede, 1980). Rooted in Weber's theory on the link between Protestantism and Capitalism, both cultural values have been used to distinguish more individualistic, industrialized Western societies from more collectivistic, traditional societies in developing countries (Oyserman et al., 2002). In the past decade, we have seen a growing number of studies that regard these cultural dimensions as two separate variables, especially in analyses of cultural influence at the individual level (Green et al., 2005; Triandis and Gelfand, 1998). Schwartz postulates (1990, p. 151) that we cannot promote "the mistaken assumption that individualist and collectivist values each form coherent syndromes that are opposed to one another". Individuals have both independent (individualistic) and interdependent (collectivistic) self-constructs (Singelis, 1994). So, they can be highly individualistic and less collectivistic or vice versa, and they can be high or low on both value dimensions (Green et al., 2005). The intensity of individualistic and collectivistic values is also dependent on social contexts (Hui, 1988; Matsumoto et al., 1997). Regarding individualism and collectivism as two independent dispositions of the founder, the question of their contribution to new venture financing arises.

4.2.1 Individualistic Values

Individualism is associated with a set of values such as competition, enjoyment, an exciting and varied life, self-reliance, social recognition, imagination, and broad-mindedness (Morris and Schindehutte, 2005). As cultural theories show, values are reflected in behavior (Schwartz, 1992). In an entrepreneurial context, individualistic values may be manifested in a higher proclivity to create new ventures, to innovate and to be oriented toward material goals: "Individualism gives rise to *entrepreneurial* behavior and a greater supply of individualism leads to greater levels of entrepreneurial outcomes" (Tiessen, 1997, p. 372). Founders with an individualistic profile are usually driven by the opportunity "to lead rather than follow" (Huisman, 1985, p. 13). Shane (1993) reports a positive effect of individualistic orientation of entrepreneurs on innovation (in terms of patents). We may therefore assume that founders with higher levels of individualistic values will be engaged in growth-oriented ventures and thus motivated (and coerced) to invest more own capital as well as capital from external sources.

In the comparative country context, it is important to stress that the Polish capital market is in the very early stage of development when compared to the situation in established market economies (Baclawski et al., 2005; Sammer and Schneider, 2006). Also the Polish banking system has been opened to private enterprises during the past fifteen years, so that the interaction between banks and new private ventures is relatively new in a post-communist context and is characterized by limited confidence (Feakins, 2004). Even though individualistic founders may want to invest in growth oriented, innovative ventures, we may expect that they will encounter difficulties when looking for funds. Hence, we may expect that a highly individualistic orientation of founders in Poland will not necessarily enable them to involve external investors with high capital and found ventures with higher levels of initial capital. Therefore, we hypothesize that:

Hypothesis 2a: *There will be a positive correlation between the individualistic values of the founder and initial financial capital.*

Hypothesis 2b: *The relationship between the individualistic values of founders and initial financial capital in a mature economy will be stronger than that of their counterparts in a transition economy.*

We also expect that the individualistic values of the founder will have an indirect effect on initial financial capital via entrepreneurial skills. Because individualistic-oriented persons strive to be independent and are likely to be creative and achievement-oriented, it may be assumed that founders who reflect strong individualistic values have a greater ability than others to recognize promising (innovative) business opportunities and to assemble crucial resources (Mitchell et al., 2000). The latter primarily reflects their stronger willingness to have a control over people and resources (Schwartz, 1992). Thus, founders with strong individualistic orientation will have a greater ability to take advantage of a new business idea.

Pertaining to potential differences in the impact of individualistic values on entrepreneurial skills in the context of different countries, the particular history of post-communist societies must be taken into account. First, in communist times, people were rather effective at organizing resources and influencing people – mainly driven by the desire to supplement the scarce supply of goods that could be obtained on the official market. Hence, entrepreneurial abilities were developed rather as a consequence of necessity, and not as a consequence of individualistic values. Second, individualist values themselves were not – at least officially – held in high regard (Tang, 1983) and may, as a result, have been underdeveloped. Therefore, we hypothesize that:

Hypothesis 3a: *There will be a positive correlation between individualistic values and entrepreneurial skills of the founder.*

Hypothesis 3b: *The relationship between the individualistic values of founders and entrepreneurial skills in a mature economy will be stronger than that of their counterparts in a transition economy.*

4.2.2 Collectivistic values

Collectivism is associated with values like cooperation, group norms, equality, stability of relationships, honesty, politeness, safety, and harmony (Green et al., 2005; Grimm et al., 1999). Central to collectivism is the belief that the self is interdependent with some in-groups (e.g. family, organization) (Oyserman et al., 2002). For collectivists, the goals of the group are at least as important as the personal goals (Parkes et al., 2001). Therefore, persons with a more collectivistic orientation value harmonious relationship with others and they try to fulfill their expectations.

Founders with a strong set of collectivistic values may prefer not to stick out from their peer group. In addition to that, their collectivistic orientation may be reflected in a higher risk aversion (striving for safety). As a consequence, it can be assumed that they favor low-growth, imitative ventures rather than high-growth, innovative ventures. To the degree that the former require a lower amount of funding, there will be a negative correlation between the collectivistic values of the founder and initial financial capital.

Looking for potential differences in the effects of collectivistic values on startup finance, we have to consider the fact that Poland is a young free-market economy with a short entrepreneurship tradition. Contrary to established market economies that abound with entrepreneurial models, this occupational choice continues to be viewed as very risky and is still not appreciated in Polish society. These social norms may hamper the realization of an innovative venture idea, so founders with collectivistic values who place a higher value on social acceptance will be more careful with courageous, capital-intensive business ideas in less friendly environments of this kind. We may expect that:

Hypothesis 4a: *There will be a negative correlation between collectivistic values of the founder and initial financial capital.*

Hypothesis 4b: *The relationship between collectivistic values of founders in a transition economy and initial financial capital will be stronger than that of their counterparts in a mature economy.*

In addition to that, we look for *alternative* interaction patterns pertaining to the relationship between collectivism and financial capital. In particular, we take into consideration the fact that founders with a collectivistic orientation value harmonious relationships.

Founders usually rely on finance resources obtained from their personal networks, i.e. from family and friends (Brüderl and Preisendörfer, 1998). A collectivistic orientation expressed by striving for harmonious and stable relationships with others may enable founders to receive more capital from strong ties. In this respect, collectivism may be viewed as a proxy for networking skills and thus as a supportive embodied tool to receive needed capital from other persons. Tiessen (1997, p. 368) underlines that collectivism enhances leverage of organizational resources "by leading to *efficient* internal and external relations".

Contrary to the situation in households in established market economies, we have to account for a considerably lower level of financial capital accumulated through generations in households in post-communist countries (Schwarz and Wdowiak, 2006). In transition economies, even if founders express collectivistic values and thus strive for harmonious and confidential relationships with family members and friends, they will not necessarily be able to use those contacts to increase startup finance due to the scarcity of that resource. We therefore hypothesize that:

Hypothesis 4c: *There will be a positive correlation between collectivistic values of the founder and initial financial capital.*

Hypothesis 4d: *The relationship between collectivistic values of founders in a mature economy and initial financial capital will be stronger than that of their counterparts in a transition economy.*

We also expect that the collectivistic values of the founder will have an indirect effect on initial financial capital via entrepreneurial skills. Collectivistic values, especially placing an emphasis on harmonious interpersonal relationships, good communication, and group needs, are reflected in a greater ability to create and maintain contacts with others and in a greater ability to identify people's wishes (Tiessen, 1997). The aptitude to build and use relations with others as well as to identify the goods and services people want constitute relevant components of entrepreneurial skills (Chandler and Hanks, 1998).

Due to the fact that a collectivistic orientation prevailed in the communism system (Tang, 1983), its cultural dimensions may still be strongly internalized within individuals in Poland. Its contribution to the development of abilities to build efficient and stable relations with others may thus be greater in a transition context. In less collectivist societies, efficient relations are often the result of rational consideration and not tacit choices linked with collectivistic orientation. Therefore, we hypothesize that:

Hypothesis 5a: *There will be a positive correlation between collectivistic values of the founder and entrepreneurial skills of the founder.*
Hypothesis 5b: *The relationship between collectivistic values of founders in a transition economy and entrepreneurial skills will be stronger than that of their counterparts in a mature economy.*

4.3 The Effects of Knowledge

The final component of Bourdieu's concept of cultural capital to be considered in our analysis is knowledge. One of the major types of knowledge in cultural concepts is procedural knowledge that comprises cognitive representations of how to achieve a particular result (Chiu and Hong, 2006). It consists of a learned sequence of responses to a situation. Through experience a learned response sequence may become a routine. Activation of a procedural representation in a given situation may thus facilitate individual behavior and performance. In a startup finance context, we shall consider knowledge acquired through industry, leadership, and founding experience. As the literature review shows, these kinds of capital have been extensively researched in a new venture financing context (see Section 3). Therefore, we will only briefly discuss the expected effects here.

From the founders' perspective, we may expect that all forms of experience, i.e. industry, leadership, and business founding, provide valuable knowledge on how to act within a specific industry, how to influence and lead people, and how to organize and manage a firm respectively. We can expect that founders who possess more knowledge and are conscious of their superior capabilities will be more likely to perceive a higher success chance and thus they will invest more of their own financial resources and search more intensively for outside finance (Carter and Van Auken, 1990).

We expect country differences in reference to industry experience. Knowledge regarding industry may open additional ways to finance new venture such as supplier credits. In Austria, trade credits as a form of startup financing is well developed (Sammer and

Schneider, 2006). In Poland, less stable institutional environments as well as criminal business practices decrease partners' trust and willingness to provide credit. Consequently, this financing alternative remains rather closed to the Polish founders. Therefore, we hypothesize:

Hypothesis 6a (1-3): There will be a positive correlation between (1: industry, 2: leadership, and 3: founding) experience and initial financial capital.

Hypothesis 6b: The relationship between industry experience of founders and initial financial capital in a mature economy will be stronger than that of their counterparts in a transition economy.

Finally, we expect that past work experiences of the founder will have an indirect effect on initial financial capital via entrepreneurial skills. With respect to industry experience, we assume that possessing industry-related knowledge facilitates the recognition of high-quality business opportunities. Founders who possess industry experience have developed capabilities specific to a particular market that enable them to adjust their venture-related decisions to the market's requirement and thus to better exploit new business ideas. Leadership experience primarily provides knowledge on how to influence people, a crucial component of entrepreneurial skills. Even if founders start their venture without employees, they contact potential investors and customers to convince them of the new business. A superior ability to influence people may be helpful in that business situation. Finally, founding experience – both of success and failure – will provide the entrepreneur with guidance on how to organize a new venture (Westhead et al., 2003). Thus, we may expect that founders' knowledge accumulated through these work experiences will enhance their entrepreneurial skills. The ratio of interchangeability between experience and skills should not be different comparing both countries (Schwarz et al. 2009). Thus, this issue has been excluded from the analysis. We hypothesize:

Hypothesis 7 (1-3): There will be a positive correlation between (1: industry, 2: leadership, and 3: founding) experience and entrepreneurial skills.

5 Methodology

5.1 Population and Sample

We test our hypotheses in two countries at different stages of economic development: Austria and Poland. Austria with a Gross Domestic Product per capita of 36,980 US$ in 2005 (World Bank, 2006) represents mature economies with a resources-rich and stable institutional environment. Poland with a GDP per capita of 7,943.34 US$ in 2005 represents medium advanced transition economies.

The research is based on a written survey carried out among new ventures created on average six months before collecting the data. All business owners of these start-ups were contacted and received a postal questionnaire in January 2007. To analyse the effects of the values and skills of a single founder on initial financial capital, we only included individual enterprises and did not sample team foundings.

In Poland a random sample of contact data for 3,203 new enterprises was provided by the National Statistical Office. 196 questionnaires from team and solo foundations (6.1%) were returned. We had to filter out new ventures founded before and after the appropriate date (data cleaning process) and exclude all team-foundations and all takeovers so that 136 cases could be used for further analysis. In Austria the contact data for new ventures was provided by the Chamber of Commerce, where all enterprises have to be registered. In the period between January and September 2006 1,813 new businesses were founded (population). 211 out of 1,813 questionnaires (11.6%) were returned. After the exclusion of team-foundations and takeovers, 127 single-entrepreneur enterprises remained for further analysis.

The Chi-square-test for differences between population and returned questionnaires concerning legal form and industry shows no significant test results in both countries. Hence, there is no bias in the sample regarding these criteria. Due to the lack of additional data on the population, further analysis of representativeness of the sample could not be carried out.

5.2 Operationalization

The initial financial capital was measured by a 9-point ordinal scale of a single item. The entrepreneurs have to state the amount of available initial financial capital. For comparison reasons, we used the scale applied in the questionnaires of the Global Entrepreneurship Monitor. The response categories of initial financial capital were: "less than 1,000 Euro", "between 1,001 and 2,000 Euro", between 2,001 and 3,000 Euro", "between 3,001 and 5,000 Euro", "between 5,001 and 7,000 Euro", "between 7,001 and 10,000 Euro", "between 10,001 and 20,000 Euro", "between 20,001 and 50,000 Euro", "more than 50,000 Euro".

Entrepreneurial skills of the founder were measured by eight items on a six-point Likert-scale, based on the scale provided by Chandler and Hanks (1998). We asked the founders to assess their abilities to recognize and take advantage of business opportunity, e.g. to seize high quality business opportunities, organize resources and coordinate tasks, or influence and lead people.

With respect to cultural values, we adapted scales from the Short Schwartz's Value Survey (Schwartz, 1992; Lindeman and Verkasado, 2005) that refers to individualism (e.g. hedonism, stimulation, and self-direction) and collectivism (e.g. security, conformity, and benevolence). Each construct was composed of six items on a six-point Likert-scale.

The internal reliability of applied constructs was tested by Cronbach-Alpha where we achieved values above the appropriate threshold of 0.7 for all constructs. The value of Cronbach-Alpha for the entrepreneurial skills scale with eight items is about 0.817. The values of Cronbach-Alpha for collectivistic and individualistic values scales are 0.736 and 0.724, respectively. Thus, internal reliability for all constructs is given. For all constructs, we calculated item mean scores for each entrepreneur.

Knowledge examined in our research was related to work experience, i.e. industry, leadership and founding experience. Each of the three items was measured on a six-point ordinal scale from "no experience", "less than one year", "one to three years", "four to six years", "seven to ten years" and "more than ten years".

We controlled the regression analysis with regard to the age of the entrepreneur measured in years, industry measured on a 3-point nominal scale and country. The industries of the new ventures were aggregated in the three categories "production", "sale" and "service" industries. We controlled for industry in our regression models by including two dummy variables representing "sale" and "service" industries. The "production" industry is the reference category in the regression analysis.

To control for country differences, we included a dummy variable for Poland in the model. The variable is 1 if the enterprise is located in Poland and 0 if the enterprise is in Austria. Hence, Austria is the reference country.

5.3 Method

According to the numeric scale of the response "entrepreneurial skills", we use a hierarchical multiple linear regression model to test the Hypotheses three, five and seven. The regression analysis is done in three steps. First we estimate a basic model with control variables for the age of the entrepreneur and the country of the firm as well as industry, leadership and entrepreneurship experience. Second collectivistic and individualistic values are included in the model to show the additional effect of the explanation of individualistic and collectivistic values on entrepreneurial skills. Third the interaction effects of all exploratory variables with the country dummy are included to test for significant country differences (Hardy, 1993). Thus, a significant coefficient of the interaction term indicates country difference between Austria and Poland.

We tested Hypotheses one, two, four and six with an ordinal logistic regression model. The selection of this method is based on the fact that we measured "initial financial capital" on an ordinal scale with varying breadth of the categories so that OLS would not be appropriate. According to this type of data, we applied an ordinal logistic regression model (proportional-odds model, parallel regression model) to estimate the relationships with initial financial capital which is based on the cumulative response probabilities. An assumption of the model is that the regression coefficients for the model are the same for each response level (parallel response assumption). Hence, the models for different response levels differ only in the intercept terms (Agresti, 2002; Fox, 1997).

We also estimated the ordinal logistic regression model in three steps. First the basic model was estimated with the age of entrepreneur, industry and the country dummy as well as the three measurements of experience. Second the variables for collectivistic values, individualistic values and the entrepreneurial skills were added, to show whether the model improves. Third we included interactions of all exploratory variables with the country dummy to test for different country effects (Hardy, 1993).

6 Results and Discussion

6.1 Descriptives

At the business level, our descriptive statistics show no significant differences between Austrian and Polish start-ups concerning industry sector. However, on the personal level, we note a few significant differences. Founders in Poland are on average three years younger than those in Austria. The mean age of the founders in Austria is 39.5 years,

Table 4. Descriptive statistic and test for country differences

	Austria		Poland			
	n	%	n	%	p-value	
Production	28	16.5	28	16.8		
Sale	20	11.8	29	17.4		
Services	79	46.5	79	47.3	0.510	
	mean	s.d.	mean	s.d.	p-value	
Age	39.47	8.94	35.99	10.78	< 0.001	***
Unemployment	2.55	1.98	3.39	2.11	< 0.001	***
Recognized business opportunity	4.41	1.50	4.87	1.50	0.015	**
Wish to realize own business idea	4.89	1.40	4.69	1.64	0.158	
Frustration in former job	2.93	1.92	2.73	2.13	0.364	
Necessity to ensure existence of the family	2.84	1.94	4.09	2.03	< 0.001	***

Tests for country differences: Chi-square test for industry, Welch Two Sample t-test for age and Mann Whitney U-test for motives
Level of significance: ** p < 0.01; *** p < 0.001

whereas the mean age in Poland is 36.0 years. Differences among the two countries exist also in the pre-founding state of employment, with more entrepreneurs starting their business from self-employment in Austria than in Poland. Findings of the pre-founding state of employment are consistent with results of the motives for establishing a business. In both countries, entrepreneurs create new ventures largely in recognition of a business opportunity. Polish entrepreneurs are more likely than Austrians to start new businesses because they were unemployed or needed to ensure the survival of their family (Table 4).

6.2 Model Results

The F-statistic for the basic linear regression model for entrepreneurial skills indicates the model relevance and also that the hypothesis that all parameters equal zero has to be rejected. The value of the adjusted R-squared reaches 0.123. Hence, 12.3% of the variance of entrepreneurial skills can be explained by this model. The extension of the basic model with collectivistic and individualistic values leads to an improvement of the R-squared measure of about 0.179 and to an explanation of entrepreneurial skills with an adjusted R-squared of 0.299. The final model with the country dummy interaction leads to an adjusted R-squared of about 0.308. Variables with no significant relationship in the final model were eliminated in all models to arrive at a simple model (Table 5).

The regression results of the basic model for entrepreneurial skills indicate that age, leadership experience and founding experience are significant on the level of 0.1% and 5%. Hence, Hypotheses 7(2) and 7(3) have to be accepted for leadership and founding experience. However it has to be noted that founding experience is only significant to a level of 10% in models 2 and 3. Industry experience shows no significant relationship in the basic model. Hypothesis 7(1) has to be rejected for industry experience. The param-

Table 5. Regression results for entrepreneurial skills

	Model 1			Model 2			Model 3		
	Estimate	t-value		Estimate	t-value		Estimate	t-value	
Intercept	4.684	22.846	***	2.038	5.344	***	1.384	2.791	**
Age	-0.022	-4.112	***	-0.017	-3.547	***	-0.018	-3.646	***
DummyPoland	0.027	0.259		0.086	0.895		1.136	2.173	*
Leadership experience	0.154	5.294	***	0.132	5.022	***	0.139	5.286	***
Founding experience	0.070	1.980	*	0.054	1.687	#	0.055	1.731	#
Collectivistic values				0.185	3.218	**	0.177	3.085	**
Individualistic values				0.370	6.642	***	0.516	5.699	***
LandPol: Individualistic							-0.229	-2.044	*
F-statistic	9.994		***	19.230		***	17.290		***
R-squared	0.137			0.316			0.327		
adj. R-squared	0.123			0.299			0.308		
R-squared Difference				0.179			0.011		
AIC	605.260			549.591			547.316		

Linear regression model with dependent variable: Entrepreneurial skills
Number of observations: 257
Level of significance: # p < 0.1; * p < 0.05; ** p < 0.01; *** p < 0.001

eter estimates of collectivistic and individualistic values in the extension of the basic model are both significantly positive on a high level. Therefore, Hypotheses 3a and 5a can be accepted. The test for country differences with the inclusion of the interaction terms with the country dummy variable results in only one significant parameter. One significant interaction term shows that there are differences in the relationship between entrepreneurial skills and individualistic values in Austria and Poland. The parameter of the interaction term is significantly negative on the level of 5%, thus the relationship in Austria (0.516) is much stronger than in Poland (0.516 - 0.229 = 0.287). So, H3b has to be accepted. The last interaction was not significant and was removed from the final model. Hence, Hypothesis 5b must be rejected (Table 5).

We also estimated the ordinal logistic regression model for the initial financial capital in three steps. We included two dummy variables in the basic model to control for industry and one dummy variable for country. In addition we controlled for age of the founder and included industry, leadership and founding experience. We removed all variables from the final model formulas which show no significant effect on initial financial capital in one out of three models in order to arrive at the simplest model.

The likelihood-ratio test (LR-test) between the basic model and the null-model with only the intercept terms show an improvement which is highly significant. In the basic model only the dummy variable for service and the country dummy show significant relationships with initial financial capital. These results indicate that there are differences in the level of initial financial capital between service and production industries and that there are differ-

Table 6. Regression results for initial financial capital

	Model 4			Model 5			Model 6		
	Estimate	t-value		Estimate	t-value		Estimate	t-value	
DummySale	-0.051	-0.147		-0.040	-0.116		-0.033	-0.094	
DummyService	-0.853	-2.849	**	-0.894	-3.007	**	-0.900	-3.027	**
Age	0.009	0.762		0.018	1.457		0.023	1.888	#
DummyPoland	-1.330	-5.372	***	-1.278	-5.029	***	0.262	0.510	
Industry experience	0.012	0.194		0.008	0.119		0.229	2.509	*
Collectivistic values				-0.298	-1.986	*	-0.269	-1.781	#
Entrepreneurial skills				0.655	4.438	***	0.631	4.259	***
Industry experience: DummyPoland							-0.422	-3.408	***
log-Likelihood	-501.809			-491.280			-485.396		
LR-Test to the simpler model	76.626	***		21.058	***		11.768	***	
DF	13			15			16		
AIC	1,029.617			1,012.560			1,002.792		
Pseudo R-squared: Nagelkerke	0.162			0.230			0.266		
Cox & Snell	0.159			0.226			0.261		

Proportional–odds model with dependent variable: Initial financial capital
Number of observations: 253
Model intercepts for different response levels omitted
Level of significance: # p< 0.1; * p < 0.05; ** p < 0.01; *** p < 0.001

ences between Poland and Austria. The initial financial capital is lower in service industries compared to the production industries and is higher in Austria than in Poland (Table 6).

The extension of the basic model with collectivistic and individualistic values and entrepreneurial skills leads to two significant parameter estimates. Collectivistic values have a significant negative and entrepreneurial skills have a significant positive relationship with initial financial capital. Hence, the findings support Hypotheses 1a and 4a (Hypothesis 4c is rejected). Individualistic values showed no significant effect and were eliminated from the final model formulas. Therefore, Hypothesis 2a is not supported. Nevertheless, the significant effects of both collectivistic and individualistic values on entrepreneurial skills, as well as the significant impact of collectivistic orientation on initial financial capital confirm our assumption that cultural investments may extend the explicatory power of human capital in the analysis of new venture creation.

To test for country differences interaction effects with the country dummy variable were included in the third step of the estimation process. The inclusion of interaction terms results in one significant negative coefficient for the interaction with industry experience. In addition, the main effect of industry experience, which was not significant in the first two steps, is now significantly positive to a high degree. This means that there are strong differences in the effect of industry experience on initial financial capital between Austria and Poland. In Austria the model indicates a positive relationship (0.229) whereas in Poland the model shows a negative relationship with initial financial capital (0.229 - 0.442 = -0.193). Hence, Hypothesis 6b can be accepted and Hypothesis 6a is supported only for Austria, because the estimated relationship for industry experience in Poland shows the inverse direction. The relationships between leadership and founding experience with initial financial capital were not significant. The variables were removed from the final model formulas and therefore Hypothesis 6a has to be rejected for these kinds of experiences. Also the interaction effects of individualistic values, collectivistic values and entrepreneurial skills with the country dummy show no significant relationship to initial financial capital, thus Hypotheses 1b, 2b, 4b, and 4d have to be rejected (Table 6). The results are summarized in Table 7 and Table 8.

Table 7. Hypotheses on Cultural Capital: Summary

	Relationship	Hypothesis	Result
H1a	entrepreneurial skills → initial financial capital	+	+
H2a	individualistic values → initial financial capital	+	n.s.
H3a	individualistic values → entrepreneurial skills	+	+
H4a	collectivistic values → initial financial capital	−	−
H4c	collectivistic values → initial financial capital	+	−
H5a	collectivistic values → entrepreneurial skills	+	+
H6a(1)	industry experience → initial financial capital	+	+
H6a(2)	leadership experience → initial financial capital	+	n.s.
H6a(3)	founding experience → initial financial capital	+	n.s.
H7(1)	industry experience → entrepreneurial skills	+	n.s.
H7(2)	leadership experience → entrepreneurial skills	+	+
H7(3)	founding experience → entrepreneurial skills	+	+

+ positive influence; − negative influence; n.s. non-significant

Table 8. Hypotheses on Country Differences: Summary

	Relationship	Hypothesis (stronger influence in)	Result
H1b	entrepreneurial skills → initial financial capital	transition economy	n.s.
H2b	individualistic values → initial financial capital	mature economy	n.s.
H3b	individualistic values → entrepreneurial skills	mature economy	+
H4b	collectivistic values → initial financial capital	transition economy	n.s.
H4d	collectivistic values → initial financial capital	mature economy	n.s.
H5b	collectivistic values → entrepreneurial skills	transition economy	n.s.
H6b	industry experience → initial financial capital	mature economy	+

+ positive influence; − negative influence; n.s. non-significant

7 Conclusions and Implications

In this study, we explored effects of cultural values (individualistic and collectivistic values), knowledge acquired through work experience and entrepreneurial skills upon the amount of initial financial capital, based on the theory of cultural capital. Furthermore, we tested the model in Austria and Poland.

We found that cultural capital affects the financing of new ventures. In particular, collectivistic values, entrepreneurial skills and industry experience have a significant impact on the amount of initial financial capital. Whereas skills and experience affect initial financial capital positively, collectivistic values have a negative influence upon the amount of startup finance. We suppose that founders with a strong set of collectivistic values favor low-growth, imitative ventures rather than high-growth, innovative (capital intensive) ventures due to the fact that they tend not to stick out from their peer group and strive for safety. In our study, we also wished to acknowledge alternative explanations. Specifically, we considered that collectivism is expressed by harmonious and stable relations with others and expected that this aspect will enable founders to rely on their personal networks to increase startup finance. Thus, we hypothesized a positive relationship between collectivistic values of the founder and the amount of initial financial capital. As stated, we observed opposing effects. Pertaining to individualistic values, we found no significant effects. We assumed that founders with a greater individualistic orientation will be engaged in growth-oriented ventures and thus motivated to invest more capital. This assumption can primarily be traced back to the fact that individualistic people tend to lead and not to follow. It is possible that individualistic orientation is more relevant in later phases of financing (venturing) cycle.

In our research, we agreed with the cultural capital theory and grasped skills as the product of other cultural investments such as values and acquired and memorized knowledge. As expected, we found a significant positive impact of collectivistic and individualistic values as well as knowledge accumulated through leadership and founding experience upon entrepreneurial skills. We observed no significant effects regarding industry experience. This result might be traced back to the fact that knowledge gained through industry experience changes relatively often due to the industrial dynamic and is thus less enduring in comparison to knowledge accumulated through leadership and founding experience, which is "saved" through routine, thus contributing to the development of entrepreneurial skills.

In the comparative country context, we were able to detect two relevant country differences. First, the relationship between the industry experience of Austrian founders and the amount of initial financial capital proved to be stronger than that of their Polish counterparts. We suppose that Austrian founders with industry experience were given more options to finance the venture, ranging from debt capital to supplier credits. The latter alternative is rather closed to the Polish entrepreneur due to the lack of trust and willingness to provide credits on the part of business partners. This situation can quite clearly be traced back to the criminal business practices that dominate in a transition economy. Second, we found significant differences in the relationship between individualistic values of founders and entrepreneurial skills. This relationship is stronger in Austria, where there is a mature economy with a longer individualistic tradition. We presume that entrepreneurial abilities in Poland have been developed rather as a consequence of necessity (i.e. as response to the scarcity of resources), and not necessarily as a consequence of individualistic values. Individualist orientation and behavior were not held in high regard under communism and may therefore still remain underdeveloped.

However, there are some limitations that have to be considered in the interpretation of the results. First, we used the amount of financial capital as the only indicator for initial financial capital. Even though we believe that this indicator is important in the context of new venture creation, other indicators such as equity and leverage might be applied to provide a more differentiated insight into the relationship between cultural and financial capital of the founder. Second, we tested the model in only two countries. Although both countries are heterogeneous with respect to economic and cultural environment, the applicability of the model needs to include more countries in future research. Third, we excluded the occupational background of the founder's parents from the analysis. Self-employed parents usually provide their children with knowledge on how to organize and lead a firm. Though that kind of knowledge is to a certain degree shared at an unconscious level, it constitutes a valuable resource in cases where the child chooses to be self-employed in the future (Bourdieu, 1986). It should be noted that including such a variable in models is primarily reasonable in economies with a long tradition of entrepreneurship. Poland with its relatively short history of entrepreneurship might not be a suitable environment to prove whether such family-embeddedness affects the acquisition of financial resources.

We hope to contribute to entrepreneurship research by extending the discussion on the role of the founder in financing new ventures from a human capital to a cultural capital perspective. While previous research extensively dealt with the effects of the founder's experience on his or her financing decisions, other components of cultural capital were addressed only to a limited degree (entrepreneurial skills) or were wholly neglected (cultural values). Our study reveals significant effects of skills and values in the context of start-up financing. The importance of cultural capital for the acquisition of initial financial capital implies the need to look more deeply into the issue of how cultural capital affects the entrepreneurial process. For example, the issue of how cultural values impact the acquisition of strategic resources for a new venture in the context of transaction costs might be worthy of exploration. Since we could confirm the effects of collectivistic values of the founder on the accumulation of financial capital, this cultural dimension might also influence other contexts of new venture creation and performance. For example, collectivistic orientation – especially placing value on good relations with others – might be relevant in the context of a family business or team founding, where effective group work seems to be crucial to new venture performance. Including cultural characteristics of founders may be also important for lenders and investors involved in the assessment of founder's capacities.

Acknowledgements
We gratefully appreciate the financial support from the Warsaw School of Economics and the Verein zur Förderung der Wirtschaftswissenschaften der Alpen-Adria Universität Klagenfurt. We would also like to thank two anonymous reviewers for their valuable comments.

Endnotes

1 New forms of capital however usually embody past mental or social effort (Dean and Kretschmer, 2007).
2 Durkheim as the first scholar emphasized the adaptive value of culture (Chiu and Hong, 2006).
3 The term cultural capital was introduced by Bourdieu and Passeron as early as 1977 in their work "Reproduction in Education, Society and Culture". But a mature concept of cultural capital was first established in 1986 in Bourdieu's work "The Forms of Capital".
4 In "The State Nobility" (1996), Bourdieu points to the dual nature of competences (i.e. knowledge and skills). The competences of an individual have both a social dimension (status) and a "technical" dimension. On the one hand, certificates attest to a social competence and in this respect they constitute an institutionalized form of cultural capital. In later work (Bourdieu and Wacquant, 1992, p. 19), Bourdieu views formal investments such as educational credentials as *informational capital*. On the other hand, the competences refer to a "technical capacity" of an individual and thus to an embodied form of cultural capital.
5 Bourdieu contends that, beyond some shared terminology, he actually has little in common with human capital theorists (Bourdieu and Wacquant, 1992). Becker has informally discussed with him the (dis)similarities of both theories (Swartz, 1997).
6 Bourdieu's critique of the human capital theory corresponds with previous critical assertions of economists who argued that "it is virtually impossible to make sense of the economics of human development (...) using a model which fails to recognize that families and schools teach different thinks" (Bowles and Gintis, 1975, p. 79).
7 In our research, we view "abilities" and "skills" synonymously.
8 International recognized journals constituting the foundation for our literature analysis are: Entrepreneurship and Regional Development, Entrepreneurship: Theory and Practice, Journal of Business Venturing, Journal of Small Business Management, and Small Business Economics.

References

Agresti A (2002) Categorical Data Analysis, Hoboken, New Jersey, Wiley
Aldrich H, Zimmer C (1986) Entrepreneurship through Social Networks. In: Sexton DL, Smilor RW (Eds) The Art and Science of Entrepreneurship. Cambridge/MA, Ballinger Publishing, 2–23
Alsos GA, Isaksen EJ, Ljunggren E (2006) New Venture Financing and Subsequent Business Growth in Men- and Women-Led Businesses. Entrepreneurship: Theory and Practice 30(5):667–686
Atran S, Medin DL, Ross NO (2005) The Cultural Mind: Environmental Decision Making and Cultural Modeling within and across Populations. Psychological Review 112:774–776
Baclawski K, Kozerga M, Zbierowski P (2005) Global Entrepreneurship Monitor. National Report Poland 2004. Katowice, University of Katowice
Bates TM (1990) Entrepreneur Human Capital Inputs and Small Business Longevity. Review of Economics and Statistics 72(4):551–559
Becker GS (1993) Human Capital. A Theoretical and Empirical Analysis with Special Reference to Education, Chicago. University of Chicago Press
Becker GS (1962) Investment in Human Capital: A Theoretical Analysis. Journal of Political Economy 70(5):9–49
Blumberg BF, Letterie WA (2008) Business Starters and Credit Rationing. Small Business Economics 30(2):187–200
Bourdieu P (1996) The State Nobility, Stanford, Stanford University Press
Bourdieu P (1986) The Forms of Capital. In: Richardson JG (Ed) Handbook of Theory and Research for Sociology of Education. Connecticut/MA. Greenwood Press 241–258
Bourdieu P, Passeron JC (1977) Reproduction in Education, Society, and Culture, Beverly Hills, Sage
Bourdieu P, Wacquant LJD (1992) An Invitation to Reflexive Sociology, Chicago. University of Chicago Press
Bowles S, Gintis H (1975) The Problem with Human Capital Theory – A Marxian Critique. American Economic Review 65(2):74–82
Bowman D (2007) Men's Business: Negotiating Entrepreneurial Business and Family Life. Journal of Sociology 43(4):385–400
Brüderl J, Preisendörfer P (1998) Network Support and the Success of Newly Founded Businesses. Small Business Economics 10(3):213–225

Bruns V, Holland DV, Shepherd DA, Wiklund J (2008) The Role of Human Capital in Loan Officers' Decision Policies. Entrepreneurship: Theory and Practice 32(3):485–506
Bruton GD, Ahlstrom D (2005) Chinese Entrepreneurship: Today and Tomorrow. In: Hitt MA, Ireland RD (Eds) The Blackwell Encyclopaedia of Management: Entrepreneurship, Oxford, Blackwell. 30–33
Bygrave WD, Hunt SA (2005) Global Entrepreneurship Monitor 2004 Financing Report. Babson, London, Babson College and London Business School
Carter RB, Van Auken HE (1990) Personal Equity Investments and Small Business Financial Difficulties. Entrepreneurship: Theory and Practice 14(2):51–60
Carter S, Shaw E, Lam W, Wilson F (2007) Gender, Entrepreneurship and Bank Lending: The Criteria and Processes Used by Bank Loan Officers in Assessing Applications. Entrepreneurship: Theory and Practice 31(3):427–444
Cassar G (2004) The financing of business start-ups. Journal of Business Venturing 19(2):261–283
Chandler GN, Hanks SH (1994) Founder Competence, the Environment, and Venture Performance. Entrepreneurship: Theory and Practice 18(3):77–89
Chandler GN, Hanks SH (1998) An Examination of the Substitutability of Founders Human and Financial Capital in Emerging Business Ventures. Journal of Business Venturing 13(5):353–369
Chandler GN, Jansen E (1992) The Founder's Self-Assessed Competence and Venture Performance. Journal of Business Venturing 7(3):223–236
Chiu CY, Hong YY (2006) Social Psychology of Culture, New York, Psychology Press
Clausen JA (1968) Socialization and Society, Boston, Little Brown and Company
Coleman JS (1988) Social Capital in the Creation of Human Capital. American Journal of Sociology 94 (Supplement), 95–120
Colombo MG, Grilli L (2007) Funding Gaps? Access To Bank Loans by High-Tech Start-Ups. Small Business Economics 29(1-2):25–46
Cooper AC, Gimeno-Gascon FJ, Woo CY (1994) Initial Human and Financial Capital as Predictors of New Venture Performance. Journal of Business Venturing 9(5):371–395
Davidsson P, Honig B (2003) The Role of Social and Human Capital among Nascent Entrepreneurs. Journal of Business Venturing 18(3):301–331
Dean A, Kretschmer M (2007) Can Ideas be Capital? Factors of Production in the Post-industrial Economy: A Review and Critique. Academy of Management Review 32(2):573–594
Farkas G (1996) Human Capital or Cultural Capital?: Ethnicity and Poverty Groups in an Urban School District, New York, Aldine Transaction
Feakins M (2004) Commercial Bank Lending to SMEs in Poland, Small Business Economics 23(1):51–70
Firkin P (2001) Entrepreneurial Capital: A Resource-Based Conceptualisation of the Entrepreneurial Process. Auckland, Massey University
Fisher I (1896) What is Capital?. The Economic Journal 6(24):509–534
Fox J (1997) Applied Regression Analysis, Linear Model, and Related Methods, Thousand Oaks, London, New Delhi, Sage
Freel MS (2007) Are Small Innovators Credit Rationed?. Small Business Economics 28(1):23–35
Green EGT, Deschamps JC, Paez D (2005) Variation of Individualism and Collectivism within and between 20 Countries: A Typological Analysis. Journal of Cross-Cultural Psychology 36(3):321–339
Grimm SD, Church MS, Katigbak MS, Reyes JS (1999) Self-Described Traits, Values, and Moods Associated with Individualism and Collectivism: Testing I-C Theory in an Individualistic and Collectivistic Culture. Journal of Cross-Cultural Psychology 30(4):466–500
Hanley A, Girma S (2006) New Ventures and their Credit Terms. Small Business Economics 26(1):351–364
Hardy MA (1993) Regression with Dummy Variables, Newbury Park, London, New Delhi, Sage
Heyman D, Deloof M, Ooghe H (2008) The Financial Structure of Private Held Belgian Firms. Small Business Economics 30(3):301–313
Hofstede GH (1980) Culture's Consequences: International Differences in Work-Related Values, Beverly Hills/ CA, Sage
Hsu DH (2007) Experienced Entrepreneurial Founders, Organizational Capital, and Venture Capital Funding. Research Policy 36(5):722–741
Hui CH (1988) Measurement of Individualism-Collectivism. Journal of Research in Personality 22(11):17–36
Huisman D (1985) Entrepreneurship: Economic and Cultural Influences on the Entrepreneurial Climate. European Research 13(4):10–17
Hutchinson J, Xavier A (2006) Comparing the Impact of Credit Constraints on the Growth of SMEs in a Transition Country with an Established Market Economy. Small Business Economics 27(2-3):169–179

Huyghebaert N, Van de Gucht L, Van Hulle C (2007) The Choice between Bank Debt and Trade Credits in Business Start-ups. Small Business Economics 29(4):435–452

Kennedy J, Drennan J (2001) A Review of the Impact of Education and Prior Experience on New Venture Performance. International Journal of Entrepreneurship and Innovation 2(3):153–169

Kilby RW (1993) The Study of Human Values, Lanham/MD, University Press of America

Kim GO (2006) Do Equally Owned Small Businesses Have Equal Access to Credit?. Small Business Economics 27(4-5):369–386

Kim H, Aldrich HE, Keister LA (2006) Access (Not) Denied: The Impact of Financial, Human, and Cultural Capital on Entrepreneurial Entry in the United States. Small Business Economics 27(1):5–22

Kluckhohn C (1962) Culture and Behavior: The Collected Essays of Clyde Kluckhohn, New York, Free Press

Kregel JA (1976) Theory of Capital, London, The Macmillan Press

Lareau A, Weininger EB (2004) Cultural Capital in Educational Research: A Critical Assessment. In: Swartz, DL, Zolberg VL (Eds) After Bourdieu. Dordrecht, Kluwer Academic Publishers 105–144

Lindeman M, Verkasado M (2005) Measuring Values with the Short Schwartz's Value Survey. Journal of Personality Assessment 85(2):170–178

Lyles MA, Saxton T, Watson K (2004) Venture Survival in a Transitional Economy. Journal of Management, 30(3):351–375

Markus HR, Hamedani MYG (2007) Socio-Cultural Psychology: The Dynamic Interdependence among Self Systems and Social Systems. In: Kitayama S, Cohen D (Eds) Handbook of Cultural Psychology. New York – London, The Guilford Press 3–39

Marlow S, Patton D (2006) All Credit to Men? Entrepreneurship, Finance, and Gender. Entrepreneurship: Theory and Practice 29(6):717–735

Matsumoto D, Weissman MD, Preston K, Brown BR, Kupperbusch C (1997) Context-Specific Measurement of Individualism-Collectivism on the Individual Level: the Individualism-Collectivism Interpersonal Assessment Inventory. Journal of Cross-Cultural Psychology 28(6):743–767

Mincer J (1958) Investment in Human Capital and Personal Income Distribution. Journal of Political Economy 66(4):281–302

Mitchell RK, Smith B, Seawright KW, Morse EA (2000) Cross-Cultural Cognitions and the Venture Creation Decision. Academy of Management Journal 43(5):974–994

Morris M, Schindehutte M (2005) Entrepreneurial Values and the Ethnic Enterprise: An Examination of Six Subcultures. Journal of Small Business Management 43(4):453–479

Ndofor HA, Priem RL (2005) Forms of Entrepreneurs' Capital, Venture Strategy and Performance. Academy of Management Conference. Honolulu

Orazem F, Vodopivec M (1997) Value of Human Capital in Transition to Market: Evidence from Slovenia. European Economic Review 41(3-5):893–903

Ou C, Haynes GW (2006) Acquisition of Additional Equity Capital by Small Firms – Findings from the National Survey of Small Business Finances. Small Business Economics 27(2-3):157–168

Oyserman, D, Coon HM, Kemmermeier M (2002) Rethinking Individualism and Collectivism: Evaluation of Theoretical Assumptions and Meta-Analyses. Psychological Bulletin 128(1):3–72

Parkes L, Bochner S, Schneider SK (2001) Person-Organisation Fit Across Cultures: An Empirical Investigation of Individualism and Collectivism. Applied Psychology: An International Review 50(1):81–107

Pindado J, Rodrigues L, de la Torre C (2006) How does Financial Distress Affect Small Firms' Financial Structure. Small Business Economics 26(4):377–391

Ricardo D (1895) Principles of Political Economy and Taxation. London: Bell

Robinson LJ, Schmid AA, Siles ME (2002) Is Social Capital Really Capital?. Review of Social Economy 60(1):1–21

Sammer M, Schneider U (2006) Global Entrepreneurship Monitor – Bericht 2005 zur Lage des Unternehmertums in Österreich. Graz

Schultz T (1961) Investment in Human Capital. American Economic Review 51(1):1–17

Schwartz SH (1990) Individualism-Collectivism: Critique and Proposed Refinements. Journal of Cross-Cultural Psychology 21(2):139–157

Schwartz SH (1992) Universals in the Content and Structure of Values: Theoretical Advances and Empirical Tests in 20 Countries. In: Zanna M (Ed) Advances in Experimental Social Psychology. New York, Academic Press 1–65

Schwarz EJ, Wdowiak MA (2006) New Venture Performance in the Transition Economies: A Conceptual Model. In: Galbraith CS, Stiles C (Eds) Developmental Entrepreneurship: Risk, Adversity and Isolation. Oxford – Amsterdam, Elsevier 89–111

Schwarz EJ, Wdowiak MA, Breitenecker RJ, Kuntaric A (2009) The Impact of Entrepreneurs' Cultural Capital on Early Performance of New Ventures: A Comparison between Austria and Slovenia. International Journal of Business and Globalisation 3(1):22–46

Shane S (1993) Cultural Influences on National Rates of Innovation. Journal of Business Venturing 8(1):59–73

Singelis TM (1994) The Measurement of Independent and Interdependent Self-Construals. Personality and Social Psychology Bulletin 20(5):580–591

Smallbone D, Welter F (2001) The Distinctiveness of Entrepreneurship in Transition Economies. Small Business Economics 16(4):249–262

Swartz D (1997) Culture and Power: The Sociology of Pierre Bourdieu, Chicago, The University of Chicago Press

Tang SH (1983) Experiments in Communism: Poland, the Soviet Union, and China. Studies in East European Thought 26(4):287–370

Tiessen JH (1997) Individualism, Collectivism, and Entrepreneurship: A Framework for International Comparative Research. Journal of Business Venturing 12(5):367–384

Throsby D (1999) Cultural Capital. Journal of Cultural Economics 23(1-2):3–12

Triandis HC (2007) Culture and Psychology. A History of the Study of Their Relationship. In: Kitayama S, Cohen D (Eds) Handbook of Cultural Psychology. New York – London, The Guilford Press 59–76

Triandis HC, Gelfand MJ (1998) Converging Measurement of Horizontal and Vertical Individualism and Collectivism. Journal of Personality and Social Psychology 70(1):118–128

Weber M (1930) The Protestant Ethic and the Spirit of Capitalism (Original work published 1904), New York, Scribner

Westhead P, Ucbasaran D, Wright M (2003) Differences between Private Firms Owned by Novice, Serial and Portfolio Entrepreneurs: Implications for Policy Makers and Practitioners. Regional Studies 37(2):187–200

Witt P (2004) Entrepreneurs' Networks and the Success of Start-ups. Entrepreneurship and Regional Development 16(5):391–412

World Bank (2006) World Development Indicators Database. Washington, World Bank

Wu Z, Chua JH, Chrisman JJ (2007) Effects of Family Ownership and Management on Small Business Equity Financing. Journal of Business Venturing 22(6):875-895

Zhang J, Soutaris V, Soh P, Wong P (2008) A Contingent Model of Network Utilization in Early Financing of Technology Ventures. Entrepreneurship: Theory and Practice 32(4):593–613

Zhang J, Wong P (2008) Network vs. Market Methods in High-Tech Venture Fundraising: The Impact of Institutional Insight. Entrepreneurship and Regional Development 20(5):409–430

Wettbewerbsvorteile durch Verzahnung von Innovation und Kommunikation!

WWW.GABLER.DE

Zerfaß, Ansgar / Möslein, Kathrin M. (Hrsg.)
Kommunikation als Erfolgsfaktor im Innovationsmanagement
Strategien im Zeitalter der Open Innovation
2009. XIV, 440 S. Geb.
EUR 59,90
ISBN 978-3-8349-1659-4

Als erstes Werk leistet dieses Buch einen Brückenschlag zwischen Kommunikations- und Innovationsmanagement. Zukunftsweisende Innovations-Konzepte werden ebenso vorgestellt wie der State of the art der Innovationskommunikation. Fallstudien namhafter Unternehmen, theoretische Perspektiven aus Sicht der Wirtschafts- und Kommunikationswissenschaften sowie empirische Ergebnisse der ersten deutschen Studie zur Rolle von Kommunikation als Erfolgsfaktor im Innovationsmanagement vermitteln einen umfassenden Einblick.

Der Inhalt
- Innovation und Kommunikation als Beitrag zur Wertschöpfung
- Open Innovation als unternehmerische Innovationsstrategie
- Strategien und Instrumente der Innovationskommunikation
- Best Practices: Innovation und Kommunikation in der Unternehmenspraxis
- Perspektiven und Herausforderungen

Die Herausgeber
Professor Dr. Ansgar Zerfaß ist Professor für Kommunikationsmanagement am Institut für Kommunikations- und Medienwissenschaft der Universität Leipzig und leitet dort die Kompetenzfelder Strategie & Wertschöpfung, Interaktive Kommunikation sowie Innovations- und Technologiekommunikation.
Professor Dr. Kathrin M. Möslein ist Inhaberin des Lehrstuhls für Betriebswirtschaftslehre, insbesondere industrielle Informationssysteme an der Friedrich-Alexander-Universität Erlangen-Nürnberg und Co-Direktorin des Center for Leading Innovation & Cooperation (CLIC) an der Handelshochschule Leipzig.

Einfach bestellen:
kerstin.kuchta@gwv-fachverlage.de
Telefon +49(0)611. 7878-626

KOMPETENZ IN SACHEN WIRTSCHAFT

Angels or Demons? Evidence on the Impact of Private Equity Firms on Employment

Eva Lutz, Ann-Kristin Achleitner

Abstract: The impact of private equity firms on employment in their portfolio companies is a controversial topic widely discussed in academia and in practice in recent years. A large body of research has resulted from this debate. The studies are focused on different aspects of employment and are based on a variety of methodologies as well as samples representing e.g. different types of buyouts and geographies. The aim of this paper is to provide access to and enhance the understanding of the highly fragmented literature by way of a systematic review and to discuss areas for future research. We review evidence on employment growth, financial and non-financial indicators of employment in a total of 49 studies. The analysis of similarities and differences of the studies shows manifold consequences of private equity on employment. Our review reveals that the impact varies across different employment indicators and between geographies. We conclude that it is not possible to label private equity firms either positively or negatively – as "angels or demons" – as this would not take account of their complex and heterogeneous effects on employees post-buyout.

Keywords: Private equity · Buyouts · Employment · Industrial relations · Systematic review

JEL Classification: G24 · L26 · J63

Acknowledgements
Special thanks are due to Benjamin Gumpp for his support in the literature search. We also thank Reiner Braun and Florian Tappeiner for their suggestions on how to improve an earlier draft. Finally, we thank two anonymous referees for their helpful comments.

Dr. E. Lutz (✉)
KfW-Stiftungslehrstuhl für Entrepreneurial Finance & Center for Entrepreneurial and Financial Studies (CEFS), TUM Business School, Technische Universität München, Arcisstr. 21, D-80333 München, eva.lutz@wi.tum.de, www.wi.tum.de/ef, research focus: venture capital and private equity, financing of family firms, company valuation, IP management, IP valuation

Prof. Dr. Dr. A.-K. Achleitner (✉)
KfW-Stiftungslehrstuhl für Entrepreneurial Finance & Center for Entrepreneurial and Financial Studies (CEFS), TUM Business School, Technische Universität München, Arcisstr. 21, D-80333 München, ann-kristin.achleitner@wi.tum.de, www.wi.tum.de/ef, research focus: venture capital and private equity, financing of small- and medium-sized companies, financing of family firms, social entrepreneurship

1 Introduction

In the late 1980s, the U.S. buyout market experienced its first major upswing in the U.S. (Kaplan/Strömberg 2008) and, as a result, a number of academic studies were undertaken to analyse the impact of private equity on employment in subsequent years. After this first wave of publications, there was less interest in this topic with only very few published studies up until 2001. However, a new discussion was started in recent years as the economic importance of private equity around the globe grew and the impact of private equity firms became more important for practitioners and policy makers alike. In 2005, a harsh public debate on private equity – the so-called locust debate – had its roots in Germany with the legendary quote from Franz Müntefering, a leading Social Democrat who later held the position of Germany's vice chancellor: "Some of these investors do not waste a thought on people whose jobs they destroy. They remain anonymous, faceless, descend like swarms of locusts on companies, devour them and move on. It is this kind of capitalism we are fighting". This prompted a broad discussion between academia, the industry, media and unions in Germany. The so-called locust debate quickly spread to the U.K. and other European countries and evolved around the accusation that private equity firms achieve exceptional rates of returns through brutal cost reductions and at the expense of employees (Davis et al. 2008). A large body of literature on the topic emerged in recent years in order to shed light on these accusations.

Theoretical explanations of the impact of private equity fall into two main categories: value transfer and value creation. The value transfer perspective explains changes post-buyout primarily based on a value shift from stakeholders of the company to new shareholders. Employees are one group of stakeholders from which a value transfer can take place (Fox/Marcus 1992; Thompson/Wright 1995). The theory is based on Shleifer/Summers 1988 who argue that value is redistributed in takeovers from employees to new equity holders as they allow to renege ex-post on implicit contracts. Their theory can be applied to buyouts as they also provide for the opportunity to renegotiate implicit contracts with employees and, thereby, to reduce high levels of employment and wages (Ippolito/James 1992). Following value transfer theory, private equity firms are expected to have a negative impact on employment as layoffs and renegotiations of wages are expected, and, in the long run, this could lead to a deterioration of trust between employees and shareholders.

Under the value creation perspective, financial, governance or operational engineering are given in the literature as main explanation for increasing company value post-buyout. In regard to financial engineering, equity is usually substituted by debt in a buyout which reduces the agency cost of free cash flow by decreasing the cash flow available for management to spend on corporate assets with zero or negative net present values or to waste it through organizational inefficiencies. The high leverage forces managers to pursue focused strategies, increase efficiencies and divest unprofitable units to generate funds to retire debt (Jensen 1986; Heinkel/Zechner 1990) which leads to an expected negative employment growth post-buyout. Governance engineering relates to activities with which private equity firms control their portfolio companies. Due to less dispersed ownership in LBOs compared to public corporations, management is monitored more closely and encouraged to maximise firm value (Jensen 1989). Operational engineering refers to initiatives to operating improvements, e.g. to improve productivity, to increase organic growth or to pursue acquisition opportunities. The external equity provided by private equity firms can be the prerequisite to pursue growth options in the portfolio company. In addition, non-financial support from private equity firms, e.g. through their industry and/or operating expertise, can help to identify growth potential or operational improvements (Kaplan/Strömberg 2008). Furthermore, operational progress can take place in a buyout through a cognitive shift to an entrepreneurial mindset and to pursue company renewal leading to revitalization and strategic innovation (Wright et al. 2001; Wright et al. 2000; Zahra 1995; Bull 1989). From a theoretical perspective, it remains unclear whether governance and operational engineering have a positive or negative impact on employment post-buyout. In the case private equity mainly enhances the opportunity to realize operational growth an increase in employment can be expected. However, in case the governance and operational engineering is targeted more towards restructuring, a negative impact on employment is likely. It is therefore not possible to draw a consistent conclusion on the impact of private equity on employment from value creation theory.

In addition to the attempts to explain the impact of private equity from a theoretical point of view, many empirical studies were undertaken on this subject. The resulting body of literature is highly fragmented as it is based on different methodologies, samples, geographies and time frames. This makes it difficult to draw common conclusions on the question of whether or not private equity firms can be labelled either positively or negatively – as "angels or demons" – when it comes down to their impact on employment-related aspects such as employment growth and other financial and non-financial indicators of employment. We want to fill this research gap by systematically reviewing evidence and, thereby, we attain a level of understanding which goes beyond that achieved in any individual study.

To our knowledge, our study is the first comprehensive review of empirical studies on the employment impact of private equity firms. There exists one systematic review by Wright et al. 2009 but it has a broader focus on the overall economic impact of private equity. In their analysis, the impact on productivity and the impact on employment and wages are two of a total of nine headings. In these two employment related sections, they outline only briefly key evidence and only take into consideration a total of 18 studies mainly from the U.S. and U.K. buyout market. Their aim is to give insights on important results without further analysing the underlying methodologies. Therefore, they do not attain our level of detail required to judge the methodologies and to understand the underlying context of different results on a variety of employment-related aspects.

Our literature review is focused on private equity investments in later stage companies, so-called buyouts. We include both private-to-private and public-to-private transactions in our analysis. To provide for a homogenous subject matter, we disregard venture capital as early stage investments in high-growth start-ups. The business model of later stage buyout funds differs fundamentally from venture capital funds, as portfolio companies of the latter are still in an early stage of their company lifecycle and, in case of survivorship, are expected to experience fast company growth leading also to high employment growth.

2 Review Framework

As described below, our systematic review of existing research follows a clear three step approach in order to allow for completeness and rigour (Tranfield et al. 2003).

Step 1: Definition of review framework
In our review framework, we cover a broad range of aspects related to the impact of private equity on employment. The impact of private equity on (I.) employment growth is investigated and includes overall growth, growth by region, net vs. gross growth and organic vs. non-organic growth. Other aspects of employment which we analyse include (II.) financial indicators and (III.) non-financial indicators. Financial indicators are wages, other forms of employee compensation and labour productivity. Non-financial indicators of employment include changes in employment structure (e.g. change from full time to part time employment), employee development and other qualitative factors influencing the work environment.

Step 2: Collection of publications
Our aim was to ensure a comprehensive, unbiased search for evidence based studies. In a first step, we used a number of keywords for an internet based search for publications. We used EBSCO Host via the Business Source Premier database, Science Direct, SSRN and Google Scholar as internet based databases for scholarly publications. We also made sure to identify publications by non-academic institutions such as national and international industry associations, auditing/consulting firms or national and international trade union organisations by screening their websites and through general web searches using Google. In addition, we found references iteratively using references cited in the already identified publications. A total number of 120 publications were identified in this step.

Our references are likely to be biased towards literature published in English, German and French due to the language skills of the authors. We cannot rule out the risk of not including publications from emerging markets, e.g. in Asia, written in native languages. However, we assume that important studies from emerging markets would have been published in English.

Step 3: Evaluation of material
The following exclusion criteria were defined in order to decide on the inclusion of the references in our review: First, publications with a focus on early stage venture capital deals (19 publications), on mergers & acquisitions in general (3 publications) and publications that did not differentiate between early and later stage investments (15 publications) were not included. Second, publications which were not based on original empirical studies such as theoretical papers (6 publications), position papers by unions (4 publications) or other descriptive publications (12 publications) were excluded. Finally, publications were excluded which do not entail detailed evidence (8 publications) or which do not offer sufficient clarity to judge the applied methodology (4 publications). This selection process led to a total of 49 publications being included in our analysis.

3 Descriptive Analysis of the Body of Literature

The 49 evidence based studies analyzed in our systematic review were published between 1983 and 2009. As shown in Fig. 1, the number of studies published over time mirrors the growth in the global buyout market. The first academic studies were undertaken in the mid-1980s when the industry was still in its infancy. The first buyout boom in the late 1980s, with the USD 25 billion leveraged buyout of RJR Nabisco (Burrough/Helyar 2004) marking its peak in 1988, led to growing interest from academia in subsequent years with seminal papers such as Jensen 1989, Rappaport 1990 and Kaplan 1991 shaping the debate on buyouts as new corporate organizational form. This period of increasing academic debate manifested itself in a first wave of academic studies on the employment impact of private equity between 1989 and 1992 (Fig. 1).

However, the bulk of studies were undertaken in a second wave, with over 70% being published post 2000. At that time, the market for buyouts experienced rapid growth both in the number and value of deals (Strömberg 2008). As Fig. 1 shows, the growth of leveraged buyouts paralleled with the second wave of publications on the employment impact of private equity. In the period 2000 to 2004, a total of six studies were undertaken with the primary focus on employment and wage growth effects. All studies published in this period were focused on European countries mirroring an upswing of buyout activity in Europe and the start of a political debate on private equity in continental Europe. The upcoming interest in the subject in continental Europe is not surprising as these countries are generally characterised by a more stakeholder oriented culture as opposed to the shareholder value approach mainly followed in the U.S. or the U.K.. The main initiators of the first studies in this second wave were European private equity associations as well as auditing and consulting firms active in the private equity market. Unions also began to compile their own fact based evidence on private equity and published studies in 2006 and 2007. In recent years, academia has shown growing interest in the employment topic. While academic studies only accounted for 25% of publications in 2003 to 2004, this figure rose to over 85% in 2008.

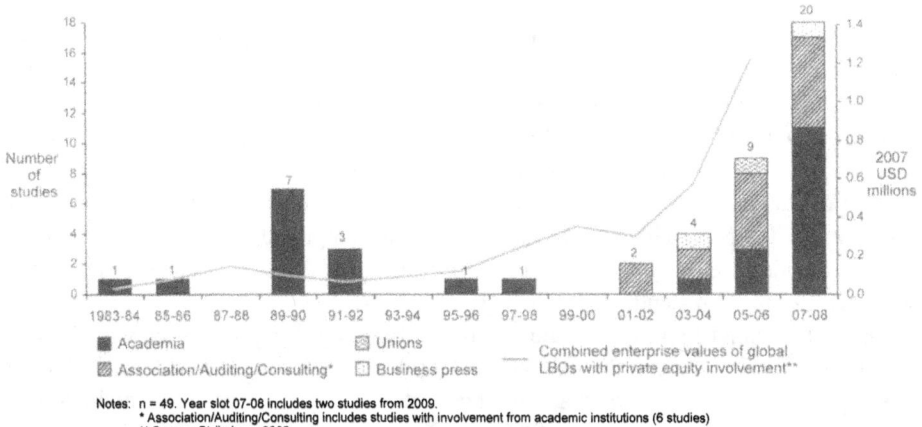

Fig. 1. Evidence based studies on employment and private equity over time

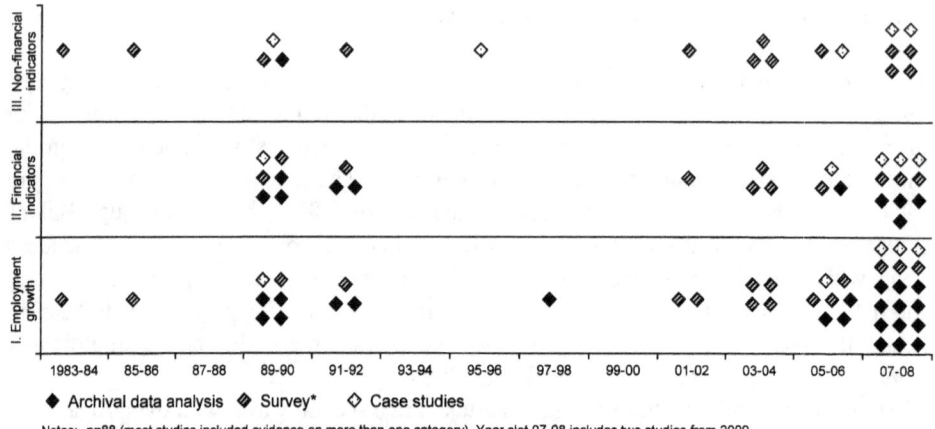

Fig. 2. Evidence based studies in each framework category over time

Fig. 2 shows how the content and methodology of publications evolved over time. After initial survey based studies in the mid 1980s, the first wave of empirical studies between 1989 and 1992 used a wide range of methodologies and covered issues in all three categories of employment aspects. The second wave of publications post 2001 again started off with studies based on surveys which were often criticized by unions and the media for small sample sizes and biases (see e.g. Hall 2007). First, questionnaire based studies suffer from a bias as only existing companies can take part in the survey leaving out unsuccessful cases of liquidated companies (survivorship bias). In addition, primarily companies with positive employment growth may participate in surveys (self-selection bias) or the numbers may be projected as more positive than they actually are (response bias). However, as we will show in the thematic analysis of the evidence in section 4, they still offer interesting insights on comparisons across different types of buyouts and on specific aspects for which no other evidence exists.

By the time period 2007 to 2008, the type of methodologies applied as well as the units of analysis became more diverse. Whereas in 2004 none of the publications were based on archival data analysis, this methodology has grown in importance and was used in 50% of studies in 2007 and over 65% in 2008. In the past two years, studies based on archival data analysis were undertaken with large samples of buyouts from the U.S. and U.K. going down to plant-level analysis of changes in employment. The increasing number of studies based on archival data analysis in recent years is linked to the increasing interest of academia in this subject. Post 2006, ten empirical studies based on archival data were undertaken with the involvement of academia, three by associations, auditing and/or consulting firms and one by the business press.

The distribution of empirical studies across different geographies is shown in Fig. 3. The bulk of studies analyze the U.S. and U.K. private equity market with studies of the U.S. and U.K. market combined amounting to 59%. For studies based on archival data analysis, the combined dominance of the two countries is even more pronounced, at 75%. This can in part be explained by data availability problems. In major continental Euro-

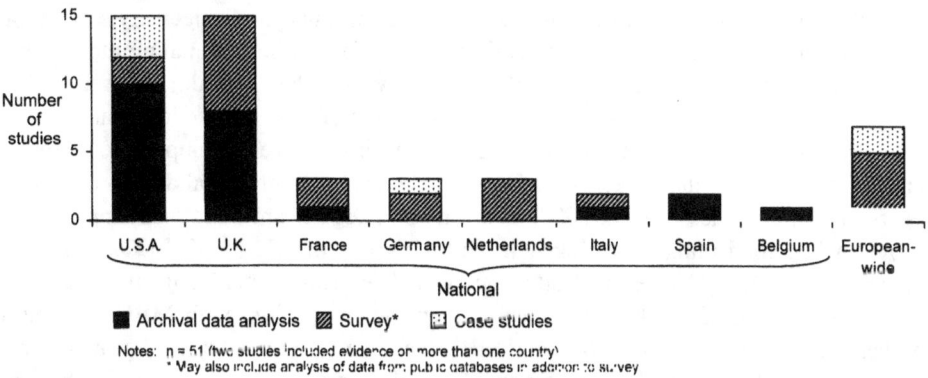

Fig. 3. Evidence based studies per region

pean countries, it is not possible to obtain reliable employment data for a large sample of privately held companies from public databases. The studies on most continental European markets therefore had to be based on questionnaires.

4 Thematic Analysis of Empirical Evidence

4.1 Evidence on Employment Growth

We identified 22 archival data based studies which show evidence on employment growth. In addition, a total of 16 survey based studies entail results on employment growth and related aspects. Furthermore, a number of case studies also offer in-depth analysis of different aspects of employment growth.

Private equity firms go through an intensive selection process in order to identify investment targets which are likely to surpass their hurdle rate of return. Portfolio companies are not chosen at random but according to their potential sources for operational or financial efficiency gains and/or growth. Therefore, the endogeneity of the investment decision has to be taken into consideration when analyzing the effect of private equity on employment (Amess et al. 2008). Evidence on changes in employment after a buyout is more meaningful if it is compared to an appropriate counterfactual.

Evidence in archival data based studies. There are different approaches in trying to take account of this endogeneity and to mirror the counterfactual in archival data based studies. First, the investment decision can be treated as endogenous dummy variable in modelling the demand for labour equation. Second, different matching algorithms, e.g. based on industry, size, productivity or company age, can be applied to construct a matched control sample. Third, an industry adjustment approach can be followed e.g. through benchmarking against industry averages or adjusting for industry effects. In reviewing our archival data based studies, we found that differing results between studies can be explained by the applied methodology to mirror the counterfactual and the underlying sample. Therefore, we grouped the archival data based studies according to their underlying methodology and we then further analyse reasons for differing results (see Tab. 1).

In the first group, we identified two studies which account for endogeneity by treating the decision to undertake a buyout as endogenous variable when estimating the demand for labour equation (Amess/Wright 2007a; Amess/Wright 2007b). Both of these studies find no significant effect of buyouts on employment from the transaction year to up to five years post transaction. In Amess/Wright 2007a, similar levels of employment growth are found in private equity-backed LBOs and in controls from the deal date to up to five years thereafter. Amess/Wright 2007b also find an insignificant impact on employment growth when controlling for endogeneity in their group of 1,350 U.K. LBOs which includes private equity-backed and other buyouts. They show significant differences for management buyouts (MBOs) and management buyins (MBIs) with MBOs having a higher average employment growth and MBIs having a lower employment growth compared to controls. The study does not yield specific findings for private equity-backed buyouts but it underlines the importance of differentiating between buyout types such as MBIs and MBOs when analyzing the impact on employment. Overall, both studies show the necessity to account for endogeneity of the buyout decision.

The second group of archival data based studies entails six studies which apply a matching strategy to construct a control sample (Amess et al. 2008; Davis et al. 2008; Cressy et al. 2008; Liebeskind et al. 1992; Marti Pellon et al. 2007; Toubeau 2006). Amess et al. 2008 use propensity matching methodology and control for pre-buyout employment growth, wages, productivity and age to construct a counterfactual control sample for 232 U.K. buyouts. They find no evidence for a significant impact of private equity-backed buyouts on organic growth of employment but show a significant negative impact on organic employment growth for buyouts without private equity sponsorship and for mergers & acquisitions compared to controls. A key difference between this study and the other studies within this group is the inclusion of pre-buyout employment growth in the matching algorithm. In other words, compared to companies with a similar employment growth prior to the transaction date, no significant impact of private equity on employment is found in portfolio companies. In case the matching algorithm does not include pre-employment growth, a significant impact of private equity can be shown. It has to be noted that the similar results of Amess/Wright 2007b, Amess/Wright 2007a and Amess et al. 2008 can potentially be an indicator of an overlap of the samples as they are all based on U.K. buyouts listed in similar databases. However, the underlying timeframe differs in these studies and, therefore, the overlap is likely to not be substantial.

Four papers find a negative impact of private equity on employment in the wake of a buyout compared to controls matched by industry, size and other factors. First, Cressy et al. 2008 analyze 57 U.K. buyouts which are matched by controls based on industry and size. Relative to controls, buyouts show 7% lower employment in the year after the transaction and higher decreases in employment up to the fourth year post-transaction. In the fifth year post-buyout, they find that relative to controls buyouts show 2% higher employment growth.

Second, Davis et al. 2008 base their matching strategy on industry, age, size and an indicator for single vs. multi-plant firms and analyze 11,000 buyouts and 300,000 plants of U.S. buyouts. Relative to controls, plants of buyouts show on average 7% higher cumulative decreases in employment two years post-buyout. Two years pre-buyout, buyout plants also have higher cumulative decreases in employment of 4% which is an indication of the endogeneity of the buyout decision. Private equity firms seem to invest in companies which have already experienced declining employment numbers in the wake of the buyout and which offer potential for further increases of operational efficiencies post-buyout. They also reveal differences depending on the industry of the investment target. Portfolio companies in retail, service, finance, insurance and real estate show a significant decline in employment whereas no significant difference was found for companies in the manufacturing sector.

As gross job creation on firm-level is equal in buyouts and controls in Davis et al. 2008, more layoffs take place in buyout firms in the wake of the transaction. The firm-level analysis also reveals that greenfield job creation is higher in buyouts, with greenfield jobs accounting for 15% of total employment, than in controls with 9% two years post-transaction. In addition, buyouts are found to be more involved in acquisitions and divestitures. Therefore, Davis et al. 2008 conclude that private equity firms are catalysts for creative destruction and accelerate contraction of less efficient activities as well as growth in new, higher value business lines.

Third, Liebeskind et al. 1992 apply matching based on industry, size and level of diversification and show that employment declined in LBOs and grew in control firms. In addition, they find LBOs to divest more business lines compared to controls and, thereby, give further evidence of private equity firms promoting creative destruction. Fourth, Acharya/Kehoe 2008 show for a sample of 66 U.K. buyouts a lower annual growth rate in number of employees compared to quoted peers in the same industry. However, the difference in employment growth is statistically insignificant.

In contrast to these four studies, we identified three additional papers based on similar methodologies but which show a positive impact of private equity on employment. These three papers use samples of buyouts in France (Boucly et al. 2009), Spain (Marti Pellon et al. 2007) and in Belgium (Toubeau 2006). Boucly et al. 2009 analyse 830 French buyouts which were closed between 1994 and 2004 and apply a matching strategy based on industry and size to construct a control sample. They show a strong increase in employment from the transaction date to four years thereafter. The employment growth in buyouts is 13% higher than in their control group. Marti Pellon et al. 2007 find average annual growth in employees in the three years post buyouts of 6.2% and an annual growth of matched controls based on location, industry and size of 2.2%. Toubeau 2006 finds significant higher increases in number of employees in buyouts compared to controls in similar industries and sizes.

The differing results of these three studies compared to the U.S. and U.K. based studies described above may be an indication that the employment impact differs depending on the institutional context, e.g. the development stage of the credit and stock markets and/or the maturity of the buyout market. Both U.S.A. and U.K. have a long history of buyout activities and can be considered to have well developed public capital market. In contrast, France, Spain and Belgium have less mature capital markets and less history in buyout activities. In these countries, private equity firms may have the role of complementing the public capital market by giving companies access to external growth finance which would otherwise be capital constrained. In more mature capital markets, companies may have better opportunities to receive growth finance from other external financing sources and, therefore, private equity firms may invest proportionally more often in companies which offer the potential of operational efficiencies rather than growth opportunities (Boucly et al. 2009). In addition, private equity firms may have more flexibility to cut employment in more shareholder value oriented cultures like the U.S. or the U.K. than in countries with a traditionally higher commitment to employees due to a more stakeholder oriented approach. This could then explain why private equity firms were found to alleviate employment growth compared to controls in countries like France, Spain or Belgium and to have a negative impact on employment in the U.S. and U.K. market.

Paper in the third group follow an industry adjustment approach in their methodology and are all based on the U.S. or U.K. market (Chaplinsky et al. 1998; Weir et al. 2008; Kaplan 1989). All of them show decreases in number of employees in buyouts relative to the industry. Chaplinsky et al. 1998 show in a study of 180 U.S. buyouts industry-adjusted mean decreases of employment of 1.8% three years and 1.7% five years post-buyout for MBOs. In analyzing 122 public-to-private transactions in the U.K., Weir et al. 2008 also find significant employment decreases in relation to industry averages in the first year post-buyout in private equity-backed companies. Kaplan 1989 separates buyouts involved in acquisitions and divestitures in his analysis of a total of 76 U.S. public-to-private transactions. In his subsample excluding companies with acquisitions and divestitures, he finds that private equity-backed buyouts reduce employment relative to the industry by 6.2% between one year prior to the transaction and one year thereafter, but his results are not significant. For the whole sample, including companies with non-organic growth, he shows significant employment decreases of 12% over the same time period relative to the industry. Smith 1990 finds significant industry adjusted reductions in employment from one year prior to the buyout to one year thereafter only for companies which have sold major parts of their assets after the transaction. The results of Kaplan 1989 and Smith 1990 stress the relevance of divestitures for changes in number of employees post buyout.

As fourth group, we found two U.S. based empirical studies which compare buyouts to randomly selected samples and, consistent with other U.S. based studies described above, both of them found higher decreases in employment in buyouts than in controls. First, Lichtenberg/Siegel 1990 analyze the employment impact on plant-level and thus measure organic employment growth only. Between one year prior to the transaction and two years thereafter, they show a cumulative decline in non-production worker employment of 8.5% in buyout plants compared to non-buyout plants. Production worker employment also declines, but less than white collar employment and not significantly so (see section 4.3). Second, Muscarella/Vetsuypens 1990 find that 92% of the random sample showed higher employment growth compared to buyouts. However, in comparison with buyouts with no acquisition and divestiture activities only 15% of the random sample showed higher employment growth.

Evidence from survey based studies. A number of survey based studies offer additional evidence on employment growth (see Tab. 2). They yield interesting insights, particularly for European countries for which archival data analysis cannot be undertaken due to the lack of data. The different studies share some common results. Many of them reveal that of the sample analyzed, between 20 and 25% of companies show a decrease in employment post-buyout (AFIC/Constantin/L.E.K. 2003; Bacon et al. 2004; CMBOR 2008; CMBOR 2004; Hanney 1986; Malone 1989; Wright et al. 1992). As mentioned above, survey based studies are likely to suffer from survivorship, self-selection and/or response bias, potentially leading to overly optimistic results in terms of employment changes. However, the results in archival data analysis based studies do not consistently show higher percentages of companies in their sample with decreases in employment compared to surveys. In terms of the average employment growth per year, the results are less consistent across different studies with a range of +2% to +13% and are likely to reveal different context factors such as geography, industry mix or time period and different backgrounds of buyouts in the sample. For instance, in the study by PWC/BVK 2005, turnarounds are excluded in the calculation of average annual employment growth of buyouts, whereas in most other studies turnarounds are included in the main sample. All of them show positive average growth rates per year across the sample that are higher than broad benchmark growth rates such as national averages or averages from comparable public companies (see Tab. 2). The results of these studies should be seen with caution not only because of the limitations due to potential biases but also because most of them originate from non peer reviewed publications.

However, insights on employment growth in different types of buyouts are revealed. Achleitner/Klöckner 2005 find the highest average annual employment growth in family firm buyouts (7.1%) compared to secondary buyouts (3.4%), going private buyouts (2.8%) as well as spin-off buyouts (1.6%) and negative average annual employment growth only in turnaround buyouts, at -3.8%. Their findings highlight the importance of the buyout background for the employment impact of private equity which could help explain the differences in results between mature and less mature capital markets as described above. It could be that in less mature capital markets private equity firms more often fulfil the role of providing external growth finance and, hence, invest more often in companies with higher employment growth than in more mature markets as these companies may be more restricted to other sources of external growth financing.

In regard to employment growth by region, a common accusation against private equity firms is that they close local entities and move them to countries with lower employment costs. Only few studies analyse the employment growth post-buyout in different regions. AFIC/Constantin 2007 reveal that 78% of all new jobs created in French buyout companies are located in France, their home country. CMBOR 2008 show that local employment increased in 26%, decreased in 7% and stayed the same in 67% of buyout companies.

Case study evidence. Case study evidence also reveals interesting findings on employment growth-related aspects. In terms of total employment growth, results are mixed and highlight the importance of the individual context of a buyout, e.g. the industry or the buyout background, for employment policies. It seems that the different case studies can broadly be divided into two groups with fundamentally different investment rationales. In one group of buyouts, the private equity firms follow a restructuring plan aiming at efficiency gains which leads to reductions in employment at least in the initial years post-buyout (examples include Messer Griesheim (Achleitner et al. 2008a), AA, Gate Gourmet, Märklin (PSE 2007), Hertz, KB Toys, Warner Music, Zeus (SEIU 2007) and Premiere (Faber 2006)). In the second group of buyouts, the investment story is based on company growth potential which is discharged post-transaction and which manifests itself in employment growth (examples are Picard, Frans Bonhomme (PSE 2007), New Look (Achleitner et al. 2008b), Onex (SEIU 2007)).

4.2 Evidence on Financial Indicators of Employment

We searched for evidence on changes in financial indicators of employment after a buyout and focused our search on changes in (1) wages and other forms of compensation, (2) employee share ownership and employee share option schemes, and (3) employee productivity. Compared to employment growth, financial indicators of employment are less frequently analyzed in the literature. We identified a total of 21 large sample studies (see Tab. 3 and Tab. 4) and a number of case studies revealing evidence on financial indicators of employment.

In terms of changes in wages and other forms of compensation, the value transfer hypothesis suggests that renegotiation of employment contracts is likely to take place post-buyout resulting in a decrease of compensation for employees. In this context, it is again important to compare wage changes in private equity backed buyouts with an appropriate counterfactual. There are only three archival data based studies which take this into account (Amess/Wright 2007b; Amess et al. 2008; Lichtenberg/Siegel 1990). Overall, they give a neutral picture in terms of the impact of private equity on wages. First, Amess/Wright 2007b control for endogeneity of the investment decision and find that buyouts lead to an increase in wages but that the increase was slightly lower compared to wage increases in their matched control sample. However, they do not differentiate between private equity backed and other buyouts. Amess et al. 2008 find that private equity-backed LBOs have no significant impact on wages, whereas buyouts without private equity sponsorship show an increase in wages in comparison with a matched control sample based on pre-buyout employment growth, pre-buyout wage growth, productivity and age. As noted above, it is likely that these two studies are partly based on the same sample but as they cover different timeframes, the overlap is expected to not be substantial. Lichtenberg/Siegel 1990 reveal a decrease in compensation for non-production workers and an increase for production workers compared to a random sample of non buyout plants. Between one year prior to the buyout and two years thereafter, annual and hourly compensation for blue-collar employees increase by 3.6% and 2.3% respectively.

In contrast to these archival data based studies, we identified a number of survey based studies which reveal a more positive view on the impact of buyouts on wages and find for the companies in their sample only a small share in which wages were reduced. As explained before, this evidence has to be viewed with caution due to potential biases in surveys. Bruining et al. 2005 analyze 145 buyouts in the U.K. and 45 buyouts in the Netherlands and find a positive impact on pay levels in both countries post-buyout. Interestingly, they do not find different impacts for the U.K. and the Netherlands. Bacon et al. 2004 find that compensation for non-managerial employees increased in 55% of buyouts in their sample of 148 U.K. buyouts, decreased in 2% and stayed the same in 43%. The studies by Bruining et al. 2005 and Bacon et al. 2004 do not distinguish between private equity-backed and other buyouts in their analysis. However, Bacon et al. 2004 acknowledge that in their survey the involvement of private equity investors lead to downward pressure on wages. It is important to notice that the U.K. survey used in Bruining et al. 2005 seems to be the same survey used in Bacon et al. 2004.

In other survey based studies, only a small percentage of private equity-backed buyouts of around 5% show a decrease in wages and about 70% have not changed compensation post-buyout (CMBOR 2008; CMBOR 2004). In an earlier study of 56 smaller company buyouts in the U.S., Malone 1989 reveals that employment contracts were renegotiated in 12% of his sample, and no change took place in 88% of his sample.

Agency theory predicts an increase in the importance of performance related pay after a buyout because the private equity firm aims to align the interests of employees with their own, i.e. with company value increases. Such a shift in types of compensation was found consistently in a number of studies. Bruining et al. 2005 show an increase in the number of staff receiving merit pay and in the number of staff whose performance is evaluated on an annual or bi-annual basis, and similar results can be found in Malone 1989, CMBOR 2001 and CMBOR/EVCA 2008. The shift to performance based forms of compensation indicates a policy change in buyouts towards increasing responsibilities of employees for their jobs and increasing pressures on employees to enhance productivity. In addition, a number of studies show an increase in other commitment-orientated employment policies such as employee share ownership or employee share option schemes. Bruining et al. 2005 and Bacon et al. 2004 find an increase in non-managerial employees owning shares in the company post-buyout. Wright et al. 1992 reveal an increase in the use of employee share option schemes with 10% of the sample introducing a scheme post-buyout and another 27% of the sample planning to introduce one. The increase in commitment-orientated employment policies could be interpreted as a shift towards a corporate culture based on an entrepreneurial mindset as it puts more emphasis on self-responsibility rather than supervision.

As described above, agency theory predicts that post-buyout efficiency gains take place in a buyout which should lead to increasing productivity. We found evidence on changes in labour productivity post-buyout in eight large sample studies and four case studies which yield consistent results and all support the hypothesis of a productivity increase (see Tab. 4). Large sample studies show increasing sales per employee (Liebeskind et al. 1992; Muscarella/Vetsuypens 1990), sales growth per employee (Deutsche Beteiligungs AG/FINANCE 2004), profits per employee (Acharya/Kehoe 2008; Weir et al. 2008; Opler 1992; Smith 1990) and an increase in total factor productivity (Harris et al. 2005; Lichtenberg/Siegel 1990) post-buyout. Consistent results on the increase in productivity were found in a number of case studies (Faber 2006; PSE 2007; Achleitner et al. 2008a; Achleitner et al. 2008b). Weir et al. 2008 also show that private equity-backed LBOs have significantly higher profits per employee post-buyout than buyouts without private equity sponsorship.

However, two studies found productivity increases in line with benchmark groups (Deutsche Beteiligungs AG/FINANCE 2004; Liebeskind et al. 1992). The different results in these studies are likely to be due to differences in the sample mix. Deutsche Beteiligungs AG/FINANCE 2004 show that for sub samples of manufacturing companies private equity backed companies show higher increases in productivity compared to the control group. Private equity funded automobile supplier companies show sales growth per employee between 1998 and 2003 of 6.7% which is higher than the increase in the control sample of 2.5%. It seems that the equivalent productivity increases in private equity backed companies and controls are due to a large proportion of service based companies in their sample. Liebeskind et al. 1992 use a sample of 33 large U.S. buyouts which were closed between 1980 and 1984. This relatively small sample of large buyouts is compared to a closely matched sample of companies with similar size, industry focus and level of diversification. Overall, productivity increases are shown in both the buyout and the control sample.

4.3 Evidence On Non-Financial Indicators of Employment

Our review also investigates evidence on non-financial indicators of employment such as changes in employee development, employment structure and other factors influencing the work environment to take account of the complexity of impacts private equity firms might have on employees. There exists only limited evidence on these indicators and we only found a total of 14 large sample studies (see Tab. 5) and a number of case studies which shed some light on changes of qualitative aspects of employment post-buyout.

Following value transfer theories, decreases in resources devoted to employees are expected post-buyout. In contrast, evidence in a number of large sample studies reveal a policy shift towards higher investments in long term employee development. Bruining et al. 2005 find an increase in investments in high commitment human resources policies and practices, suggesting that buyouts release upside growth potential rather than protecting downside risk. They reveal an increase in resources devoted to managing employees and in the amount of employee training post-buyout, but, as mentioned above, they do not distinguish between private equity-backed buyouts and other buyouts (Bruining et al. 2005). Bacon et al. 2004 show similar findings, with 55% of buyouts increasing the amount of training employees receive and only 6% showing a decrease but, as mentioned above, this study is likely to be based on the same U.K. sample as Bruining et al. 2005. Other survey based studies also reveal an increase in training expenditure post-buyout (AFIC/Constantin 2007; AFIC/Constantin/L.E.K. 2003; CMBOR 2008; CMBOR 2004; CMBOR 2001; CMBOR/EVCA 2008).

We found evidence on different aspects relating to changes in the overall employment structure in buyout companies such as part-time vs. full-time employees. Based on the value transfer hypotheses, renegotiation of employment contracts to more favourable terms for shareholders are expected which could imply a shift from full-time to part-time employment. Bruining et al. 2005 find an increase in temporary workers for their U.K. sample, whereas a decrease was revealed for their Dutch sample. These differences between the U.K. and the Netherlands can potentially be explained by the different institutional context. In the U.K., a more shareholder oriented approach may lead to lower commitment to employees compared to the stakeholder oriented approach traditionally followed in the Netherlands. The institutional context in the Netherlands is characterised by a stakeholder-oriented culture as well as strong labour legislation, high degree of trade union influence and involvement of employees through a required work council in companies with more than 50 employees. A shift towards temporary workers is therefore more difficult to pursue in countries like the Netherlands. In an earlier U.K. study, Wright et al. 1990 also find an increasing level of part-time employment post-buyout.

Other results on the overall employment structure include findings on the ratio of skilled vs. unskilled employees. Amess et al. 2007 reveal a skill-biased organisational change in favour of craft and skilled service employees after a buyout. In addition, evidence on an increase in R&D intensity post-transaction can be found in Zahra 1995 and Liebeskind et al. 1992 indicating a shift towards R&D intensive labour in buyouts.

Private equity is likely to have an impact on soft, qualitative factors of employment regarding the general work environment such as the amount of employee discretion or changes in the general working atmosphere. In a number of studies, higher employee involvement was found post-buyout. Amess et al. 2007 found an increase in employee discretion through a reduction of hierarchical tiers and supervisory staff. Lichtenberg/Siegel 1990 identify a decline in the ratio of non-production to production workers post-buyout and higher compensation of production workers which suggest a substitution of direct monitoring by higher responsibility of blue-collar employees. Bruining et al. 2005 and Bacon et al. 2004 reveal an increase in employee involvement, task flexibility and workers' responsibility after a buyout. In addition, they find an increase in the number of employees working in teams.

As explained above, consistent evidence was found on the increase in labour productivity in buyout companies. Furthermore, an increase in performance-related pay and employee share-ownership was detected in different studies. In addition to the increase in employee involvement and responsibility, these factors may imply a negative impact on the perceived work environment, as employees may feel increasing pressures to perform. We did not find a lot of evidence on changes in the work environment post-buyout. AFIC/Constantin 2007 identify an average decline in absenteeism and turnover rates but this could be interpreted both positively as a sign of increasing motivation or, at least for decreasing absenteeism, negatively as a result of increasing pressures. PSE 2007 identify an increase in working hours per week and a less positive atmosphere between work council and management. Hanney 1986 finds, at 6%, a low proportion of buyout companies that withdrew trade union recognition post-buyout and, thereby, is consistent with similar findings in other studies (Wright et al. 1990; Wright et al. 1984; CMBOR/EVCA 2008).

In addition, there is some evidence indicating changes in terms of communication policies with employees after a private equity transaction. CMBOR 2004 and CMBOR/EVCA 2008 find an increase in communication between management and employees. In the study of 50 buyouts in France by AFIC/Constantin/L.E.K. 2003, the impact on communication with employees was perceived to have changed favourably by 31% of managers, unfavourably by 8% and to have remained unchanged by 60%. However, it would be important to also investigate the opinion of employees on changes in communication as they could perceive it differently, possibly in a more negative way, compared to the managers.

5 Summary and conclusion

The aim of our paper was to systematically review evidence based research on the employment impact of private equity firms and, thereby, to increase common knowledge on the subject. We identified 49 evidence based studies and showed how the research became more sophisticated in recent years covering a broad range of methodologies and offering insights on diverse aspects of employment. Academia has become more interested in the topic and dominated the outlet of publications in the last two years. Studies are mainly focused on more mature buyout markets like the U.S. and the U.K., partly due to easier access to employment data.

In regard to employment growth, 22 archival data based studies, 16 survey based studies and 5 case studies were reviewed. At first sight, results seem to paint an inconsistent picture across the different publications. However, when the underlying methodologies and samples are analysed, the reasons for discrepancies can be explained. Papers controlling for endogeneity of the investment decision do not find a significant impact of private equity on employment. In comparison to a matched sample but not controlling for pre-buyout employment growth, studies based on the U.S.A. and the U.K. consistently find decreasing number of employees in buyouts compared to controls. Three papers which look at less mature capital markets – France, Spain and Belgium – find increasing employment post buyout compared to matched samples. This gives an indication of the importance of institutional backgrounds for the employment impact. It could be that in less mature markets private equity firms give companies access to external growth financing which would otherwise be capital constrained. In addition, different labour legislation and a stakeholder vs. shareholder oriented culture is likely to lead to different results on the impact of private equity on employment across geographies. Another important overall result on employment growth is that private equity-backed companies are found to create more greenfield jobs and are seen to be more active in acquisitions and divestitures.

In terms of financial indicators of employment, increasing labour productivity is consistently shown in different evidence based studies. The impact of private equity on wages is not extensively researched yet but the current evidence suggests a neutral role. Additional research taking account of the endogeneity of the investment decision and comparing buyouts to an appropriate counterfactual is required to better judge the impact of private equity on wages. A shift towards higher performance-related compensation and higher employee share ownership is shown which goes hand in hand with a shift towards higher employee discretion, higher employee involvement and worker responsibility post-buyout. A primarily positive impact on other non-financial indicators is shown in a number of studies with increasing funding of employee development and long term investments in the R&D size and capability. However, some qualitative indicators of employment such as the work environment have not yet been investigated enough to draw common conclusions.

In sum, our systematic review of the evidence revealed complex consequences of private equity on different aspects of employment. It would not only oversimplify the topic but would also be incorrect to view private equity firms either negatively or positively – as "angels or demons" – in terms of their impact on employment, even though enough individual studies exist to support either view for some indicators of employment. This underlines the relevance of our paper in comparing and synthesizing findings across the whole body of literature and across different indicators of employment.

Although considerable progress has been made in empirical research on the employment impact of private equity, we still see a number of research gaps. Many large sample studies as well as case study research reveal fundamental differences between types of buyouts. Although some seminal papers exist that differentiate between MBOs and MBIs, future empirical research could go beyond this and also distinguish buyouts with different backgrounds e.g. public-to-private transactions vs. private-to-private transactions. It would also be interesting to analyze more specific types of private equity investments such as buyouts of family firms or divisions of large conglomerates and their impact on employment. In addition, further research on our proposed differentiation based on the investment rationale in restructuring and growth buyouts could analyze whether dominance of either form exists.

Appendix

Tab. 1. Selected[1] archival data based studies on employment growth

Authors, Year	Peer reviewed?	Journal	Sample	Geogr.	Time	Benchmark/ Matching	Analysis	Major Findings on Employment Growth	Reg. growth	Gross growth	Organic growth
Category 1: Papers controlling for endogeneity of investment decision											
Amess/ Wright 2007b	✓	International Journal of Economics in Business	1,350 buyouts (MBI, MBO)[2]	U.K.	1999–2004	Matching based on industry and size, treating investment decision as endogenous	Simult. equation modelling	Controlling for endogeneity, insignificant effect on employment growth of LBOs (MBO & MBIs combined) Controlling for endogeneity, higher average employment growth for MBOs & lower for MBIs compared to controls	×	×	×[3]
Amess/ Wright 2007a	Not yet	Working paper	533 buyouts[2]	U.K.	1993–2004	Matching based on industry and size, treating investment decision as endogenous	Dyn. derived demand for labour equat.	Controlling for endogeneity, no significantly different levels of employment in pe & non-pe-backed LBOs than in controls	×	×	×[3]
Category 2: Papers with matching strategy											
Acharya/ Kehoe 2008	Not yet	Working paper	66 buyouts	U.K.	1996–2004	Matching with quoted peers based on industry	Difference in means and median	Buyouts grow employment at 1.6% CAGR compared to 2.7% in quoted peers, difference is statistically insignificant	×	×	×
Amess et al. 2008	Not yet	Working paper	232 buyouts[2]	U.K.	1996–2006	Propensity matching controlling for pre-buyout employment, wages, productivity, age	Multinomial probit regression	No evidence for significant impact of pe-backed LBOs on employment in t+1 or t+2 Non-pe-backed LBOs: 11% lower employment in t+1 M&A transactions: 16% lower employment in t+1, 22% lower employment in t+2	×	×	✓
Boucly et al. 2009	Not yet	Working paper	830 buyouts	France	1994–2004	Matching based on industry and size	Difference in means	Significant increase in number of employees between t and t+3, 13% higher employment growth in buyouts compared to controls	×	×	×

Tab. 1 (continued)

Authors, Year	Peer reviewed?	Journal	Sample	Geogr.	Time	Benchmark/ Matching	Analysis	Major Findings on Employment Growth	Reg. growth	Gross growth	Organic growth
Cressy et al. 2008	Not yet	Working paper	57 buyouts	U.K.	1995–2002	Matching based on industry and size	Loglinear employment regressions	Relative to controls, 7% lower employment in buyouts in t+1, cumulating to 23% lower employment in t+4; in t+5 increase by 2%	✗	✗	✗
Davis et al. 2008	Not yet	Working paper	11,000 buyouts; 300,000 plants	U.S.A.	1980–2005	Plant matching based on industry, age, size and indicator for multi-plant firm	Event study and regression analysis	7% (4%) average cumulative decrease in targets relative to controls two years post-buyout (two years pre-buyout) No employment differences between targets and controls in manufacturing sector, significant decline in targets in retail, services & finance, insurance & real estate Gross job creation equal in targets & controls; greater job destruction in targets Greenfield job creation: 15% in buyouts, 9% in controls; Acquisition (divestiture) rate: 7.3% (5.7%) in buyouts, 4.7% (2.9%) in controls	(✓)	✓	✓
Liebeskind et al. 1992	✓	Financial Management	33 public to privates	U.S.A.	1980–1984	Matching based on industry, size and level of diversification	Difference in means	Mean number of employees declined in LBOs and grew in control firms, resulting in significant differences between the samples Mean number of plants declined in LBOs and grew in control firms, resulting in significant differences between the samples	✗	✗	✗
Marti Pellon et al. 2007	✗	ASCI Research Paper	100 buyouts	Spain	1993–2004	Matching based on location, industry and size	Difference in means	In LBOs, average annual growth in employees from t to t+3 of 6.2%; in controls, average annual growth in employees from t to t+3 of 2.2%	✗	✗	✗
Toubeau 2006	✗	Doctoral thesis	53 buyouts	Belgium	1995–2005	Matching based on industry and size	Logistic regression	Significant higher increase in number of employees in buyouts compared to controls between t and t+2	✗	✗	✗

Tab. 1 (continued)

Authors, Year	Peer reviewed?	Journal	Sample	Geogr.	Time	Benchmark/ Matching	Analysis	Major Findings on Employment Growth	Reg. growth	Gross growth	Organic growth
Category 3: Papers with industry adjustment approach												
Chaplinsky et al. 1998	✓	Journal of Financial Economics	180 buy-outs (EBO, MBO)	U.S.A.	1980–1994	Adjustment for industry effects	Difference in means and median	Relative to their industry, EBOs and MBOs reduce employment after the buyout; Industry adjusted mean decrease: In t+3: -9.6% for EBOs, -1.8% for MBOs; In t+5: -10.8% for EBOs, -1.7% for MBOs	✗	✗	✗
Kaplan 1989	✓	Journal of Financial Economics	76 public to privates	U.S.A.	1980–1986	Benchmarking against industry averages	Difference in median	Total sample: Relative to their industry, MBOs reduce employment between t-1 and t+1 at -12.0%; 30.9% of sample reduce employment Excluding companies with divestitures & acquisitions: Relative to their industry, MBOs reduce employment between t-1 to t+1 at -6.2%, but results are not significant; 38.5% of sample reduce employment	✗	✗	✓
Smith 1990	✓	Journal of Financial Economics	58 public to privates	U.S.A.	1977–1986	Adjustments for industry effects	Difference in median	Relative to industry, number of employees decreases from t-1 to t+1, but insignificant Relative to industry, asset-sale sample shows significant median reductions in employment from t-1 to t+1	✗	✗	(✓)
Weir et al. 2008	Not yet	Working paper	122 public to privates	U.K.	1998–2004	Benchmarking against industry average	Difference in median	Relative to industry average, significant decrease in employment in pe-backed LBOs in t+1; further decreases in t+2 to t+5 but no significant differences to industry average Significant decrease in employment in non-pe-backed LBOs in t+1, increase in employment in subsequent years relative to industry average	✗	✗	✗

Tab. 1 (continued)

Authors, Year	Peer reviewed?	Journal	Sample	Geogr.	Time	Benchmark/ Matching	Analysis	Major Findings on Employment Growth	Reg. growth	Gross growth	Organic growth
Category 4: Other papers with control samples											
Lichtenberg/Siegel 1990	✓	Journal of Financial Economics	1,132 buyout plants	U.S.A.	1983–1986	Comparison of buy-out & non-buyout plants	Difference in means	Between t-1 & t+2, significant reductions in non-production worker employment, cumulative decline of 8.5% Production worker employment declines, but less and not significant	(✓)	✗	✓
Muscarella/Vetsuypens 1990	✓	Journal of Finance	72 public to privates	U.S.A.	1976–1987	Comparison with random sample	Difference in means	For all LBOs: Median reduction in employment between LBO and IPO -0.6%; 92% of random sample showed higher employment growth For LBOs with no acquisition/divestiture: Median increase in employment between LBO and IPO 17%; 15% of random sample showed higher employment growth	✗	✗	✓

Note: [1] The table does not include archival data based studies which do not follow a matching strategy, an industry adjustment approach or other forms of control samples (e.g. in Shapiro/Pham 2008, Taylor/Bryant 2007, Ernst & Young 2007, PWC/AIFI 2006, Marti Pellon et al. 2005). [2] Likely to be based in part on the same sample. [3] In control sample, no companies included with increases in total assets >100%. ✓ = included in analysis, (✓) = partly included in analysis, ✗ = not included in analysis. LBO = leveraged buyout, EBO = employee buyout, MBO = management buyout, MBI = management buyin.

Tab. 2. Survey based studies on employment growth

Authors, Year	Peer reviewed?	Sample	Geogr.	Time	Employment Growth			Other Major Findings on Employment Growth
					Decrease in % of Sample	Average Growth in sample	Benchmark Growth	
Achleitner/Klöckner 2005	✗	99 buyouts	Europe	1997–2004	33%	2.4% p.a.	0.7% (EU25); 0.1% (DJ 600) p.a.	Buyouts outgrew listed comp. in 6 of 10 industries; Growth p.a.: 7.1% in family firms, 3.4% in secondaries, 2.8% in going privates, 1.6% in spin-offs, -3.8% in turnarounds
AFIC/Constantin 2007	✗	94 buyouts	France	2003–2005		4.1% p.a.	0.6% p.a.	78% of all new jobs created in French buyouts are located in France
AFIC/Constantin/ L.E.K. 2003	✗	50 buyouts	France	1999–2003	20%	8.7% p.a.	2.7% p.a. (corporate labour force)	
AIFI 2001	✗	101 buyouts	Italy	1988–2000		1.6% p.a.	-1.5% p.a. (SME sample)	Employment increase prior to buyout: 1.0% p.a.; on average, 1% of employees were laid off leading to a gross growth of 2.6%
Bacon et al. 2004	✓	148 buyouts	U.K.	1998–1999	21%			
Chapman/Klein 2009	Not yet	288 buyouts	U.S.A.	1984–2006		13.4% p.a. (from t to exit)		
CMBOR 2008	✗	70 buyouts	Netherlands	1992–2005	22%			Local employment increased in 26%, decreased in 7% and stayed the same in 67% of companies
CMBOR 2005	✗	117 family buyouts	Europe	1994–2003		7.0% p.a. (from t-2 to t+2)		
CMBOR 2004	✗	46 buyouts	Netherlands	1992–2002	23%			

Tab. 2 (continued)

Authors, Year	Peer reviewed?	Sample	Geogr.	Time	Employment Growth			Other Major Findings on Employment Growth
					Decrease in % of Sample	Average Growth in sample	Benchmark Growth	
CMBOR 2001	✗	300 buyouts	Europe	2000	26%	Average: 47.5% (from to exit)		
Deutsche Beteiligungs AG/FINANCE 2004	✗	70 buyouts	Germany	1999–2003		4.5% p.a.	2.2% p.a. (control sample)	Job cuts in market downturns less severe than in control sample
Hanney 1986	✓	57 buyouts	U.K.	1980–1983	24%			
Malone 1989	✓	56 buyouts	U.S.A.	1981–1987	25%			Change in regard to elimination of rank-and-file workers post-buyout: 68% no change, 7% less, 20% more, 5% far greater emphasis
PWC/BVK 2005	✗	128 buyouts	Germany	2000–2004	5%	Median: 4.4% excl. turnar. (2000–2004)		Median decrease in turnaround buyouts: -28.6% (2000-2004)
Wright et al. 1992	✓	182 buyouts	U.K.	1986	25%	6.3% in t		In t+1, employment increased at 1.9%
Wright et al. 1984	✓	111 buyouts	U.K.	1983	44%	18.1% in t		

Tab. 3. Evidence on change in compensation

Authors, Year	Peer reviewed?	Sample	Geogr.	Method.	Time	Findings on change in compensation
Arness/Wright 2007b	✓	1,350 LBOs[1]	U.K.	ADA	1999–2004	Wage increase, but lower in all LBOs and in MBIs than in controls
Amess et al. 2008	Not yet	232 LBOs[1]	U.K.	ADA	1996–2006	No impact on wages in pe-backed LBOs, wage increase in non-pe-backed LBOs
Lichtenberg/Siegel 1990	✓	1,132 plants	U.S.A.	ADA	1983–1986	Wage increase for production employees between t-1 and t+2 at 3.5% (2.3%) annual (hourly) compensation, decrease for non-production workers
AFIC/Constantin 2007	✗	94 buyouts	France	Survey	2003–2005	Wage increase of average 3.3% p.a.
Bacon et al. 2004	✓	148 buyouts[2]	U.K.	Survey	1994–1997	Wage increase (decrease) in 55% (2%) of all buyouts, involvement of pe investors resulted in downward pressure on wages. Increase in commitment-orientated employment policies with performance-related pay and employee share ownership
Bruining et al. 2005	✓	190 buyouts[2]	UK, Netherlands	Survey	1992–1998	Increase in compensation of non-managerial employees. Increase in performance-related compensation. No change in non-managerial employees owning shares
CMBOR 2008	✗	70 buyouts	Netherlands	Survey	1992–2005	Wage increase (decrease) in 25% (3%) of sample
CMBOR 2004	✗	46 buyouts	Netherlands	Survey	1992–2002	Wage increase (decrease) in 25% (5%) of sample
CMBOR 2001	✗	300 buyouts	Europe	Survey	2000	Increase in performance-related compensation in 28% of sample
CMBOR/EVCA 2008	✗	190 buyouts	Europe	Survey	2008	Wage increase (decrease) in 51% (3%) of sample. Increase in performance-related compensation post buyout
Malone 1989	✓	56 buyouts	U.S.A.	Survey	1981–1987	Renegotiating employment contracts in 12% of sample, no change in 88%. Shift to performance-related pay in 41% of sample
Wright et al. 1992	✓	182 buyouts	U.K.	Survey	1986	Increase in use of share option scheme, 10% of sample introduced one post-buyout, 27% planned to introduce one

Note: ADA = archival data analysis. [1] Likely to be based in part on the same sample. [2] U.K. sample likely to be identical in both studies.

Tab. 4. Evidence on change in labor productivity

Authors, Year	Peer reviewed?	Sample	Geogr.	Method.	Time	Findings on change in productivity
Acharya/Kehoe 2008	Not yet	66 buyouts	U.K.	ADA	1996–2004	11.6% CAGR in EBITDA per employee vs. 5.9% in controls
Deutsche Beteiligungs AG/FINANCE 2004	✗	70 buyouts	Germany	Survey	1999–2003	Average increase in sales growth per employee at 3.0% p.a. vs. 3.4% for benchmark group Average increase in sales growth per employee p.a. in sub samples of manufacturing companies higher than in benchmark group
Harris et al. 2005	✓	979 buyouts, 4,877 plants	U.K.	ADA	1994–1998	-1.6% (-2.0%) lower total factor productivity of MBOs in the short term (long term) prior to buyout +70.5% (+90.3%) higher total factor productivity of MBOs in the short term (long term) post-buyout
Lichtenberg/Siegel 1990	✓	1,132 plants	U.S.A.	ADA	1983–1986	Increase in total factor productivity of plants from 2.0% above industry mean three years pre-buyout to 8.3% above industry in three years post-buyout
Liebeskind et al. 1992	✓	33 public to privates	U.S.A.	ADA	1980–1984	Significant increase in sales per employees in buyouts and controls between t and t+3
Muscarella/Vetsuypens 1990	✓	72 public to privates	U.S.A.	ADA	1976–1987	Median increase in sales per employee of 3.1%
Opler 1992	✓	44 public to privates	U.S.A.	ADA	1985–1989	Average increase in operating profit per employee of 31.8% from t-1 to t+2; after industry adjustment: 40.3%
Smith 1990	✓	58 public to privates	U.S.A.	ADA	1977–1986	Median increase in operating profit per employee of 41% from t-1 to t+1; after industry adjustment: 71% Median increase in operating profit per employee from t-1 to t+2 insignificant before and after industry adjustment
Weir et al. 2008	Not yet	122 public to privates	U.K.	ADA	1998–2004	Relative to t+1, significant increases in profit per employee in years t+2 and t+5 in pe-backed LBOs; Relative to industry average, significantly higher profit per employees in each post-deal year; Pre- and post-buyout, significantly better profit per employee in pe-backed LBOs than non-pe-backed LBOs

Note: ADA = archival data analysis.

Tab. 5: Evidence on non-financial indicators of employment

Authors, Year	Peer reviewed?	Sample	Geogr.	Time	Employment structure	Employee development	Work environment
Studies based on archival data analysis							
Lichtenberg/Siegel 1990	✓	1,132 plants	U.S.A.	1983–1986	Decline in ratio of non-production to production workers by 7%		
Liebeskind et al. 1992	✓	33 public to privates	U.S.A.	1980–1984	Less increase in R&D intensity in buyouts		
Survey based studies							
AFIC/Constantin 2007	✗	94 buyouts	France	2003–2005		Increase in training expenditure by 10% (as % of total payroll)	Average decline in absenteeism and turnover rates
AFIC/Constantin/ L.E.K. 2003	✗	50 buyouts	France	1999–2003		Impact on training: 26% favourable, 74% neutral	Impact on relations with employees: 31% favourable, 60% neutral, 8% unfavourable
Amess et al. 2007	✓	1959 firms, 27263 employees	U.K.	1998	Skill biased organisational change in favour of craft and skilled service employees		Reduction in hierarchical tiers and supervisory staff leading to higher employee discretion
Bacon et al. 2004	✓	148 buyouts[1]	U.K.	1998–1999		Increase (decrease) in amount of employee training in 55% (6%) of sample; Low impact of private equity firms on human resources policies	Increase in employee involvement and task flexibility; Low impact of private equity firms on human resources policies
Bruining et al. 2005	✓	190 buyouts[1]	UK, Netherlands	1992–1998	Change in the use of temporary workers: increase in UK, decrease in Netherlands	Increase in resources devoted to managing employees and in amount of employee training	Increase in employee involvement and workers responsibility; increase in total number of employees working in teams
CMBOR 2008	✗	70 buyouts	Netherlands	1992–2005		Increase in funding for training by 31% (as % of sales)	

Tab. 5 (continued)

Authors, Year	Peer reviewed?	Sample	Geogr.	Time	Employment structure	Employee development	Work environment
CMBOR 2004	x	46 buyouts	Netherlands	1992–2002		Increase in funding for training by 46% (as % of sales)	Increase in communication between management and employees
CMBOR 2001	x	300 buyouts	Europe	2000		Increase in funding for training by 54% (as % of sales)	High importance of promoting employee involvement post-buyout
CMBOR/EVCA 2008	x	190 buyouts	Europe	2008		Impact on amount spend for training: 45% of sample increase, 3% decrease	Attitude towards union remained unchanged; Increase in employee commitment through greater employee engagement, regular team briefings and harmonised terms and conditions between management and non-management
Hanney 1986	✓	57 buyouts	U.K.	1980–1983			6% of sample withdrew trade union recognition post-buyout
Wright et al. 1990	✓	182 buyouts	U.K.	1983–1986	Increasing level of part-time employment		No evidence of explicit attempt by management to remove trade unions; no declared incidence of opposition from trade unions against buyout
Wright et al. 1984	✓	111 buyouts	U.K.	1983			Low level of loss of trade union recognition; Low opposition from unions towards buyout

Note: [1] U.K. sample likely to be identical in both studies.

References

Acharya VV, Kehoe C (2008) Corporate Governance and Value Creation: Evidence from Private Equity, Working Paper, London Business School, London

Achleitner A-K, Klöckner O (2005) Employment Contribution of Private Equity and Venture Capital in Europe, EVCA Research Paper, Brussels

Achleitner A-K, Nathusius E, Herman K, Lerner J (2008a) Messer Griesheim, in: World Economic Forum (Ed.): Globalization of Alternative Investments Working Papers Volume 1 – The Global Economic Impact of Private Equity Report 2008, Cologny/Geneva, p 91–102

Achleitner A-K, Nathusius E, Herman K, Lerner J (2008b) New Look, in: World Economic Forum (Ed.): Globalization of Alternative Investments Working Papers Volume 1 – The Global Economic Impact of Private Equity Report 2008, Cologny/Geneva, p 103–111

AFIC/Constantin (2007) L'impact social des opérations de LBO en France, AFIC/Constantin Study, Paris

AFIC/Constantin/L.E.K. (2003) LBOs and Company Development in France, AFIC/Constantin/L.E.K. Study, Paris

AIFI (2001) The Economic Impact of Management Leveraged Buy-Out, AIFI Study, Milan

Amess K, Brown S, Thompson S (2007) Management Buyouts, Supervision and Employee Discretion, in: Scottish Journal of Political Economy 54(4):447–474

Amess K, Girma S, Wright M (2008) What are the Wage and Employment Consequences of Leveraged Buyouts, Private Equity and Acquisitions in the UK?, Working Paper, NUBS Research Paper Series No. 2008-01, Nottingham University, Nottingham

Amess K, Wright M (2007a) Barbarians at the Gate? Leveraged Buyouts, Private Equity and Jobs, Working Paper, Nottingham University, Nottingham

Amess K, Wright M (2007b) The Wage and Employment Effects of Leveraged Buyouts in the UK, in: International Journal of the Economics of Business 14(2):179–195

Bacon N, Wright M, Demina N (2004) Management Buyouts and Human Resource Management, in: British Journal of Industrial Relations 42(2):325–347

Boucly Q, Sraer D, Thesmar D (2009) Job Creating LBOs, Working Paper, HEC Paris, Paris

Bruining H, Boselie P, Wright M, Bacon N (2005) The Impact of Business Ownership Change on Employee Relations: Buy-outs in the UK and The Netherlands, in: The International Journal of Human Resource Management 16(3):345–365

Bull I (1989) Financial Performance of Leveraged Buyouts: An Empirical Analysis, Journal of Business Venturing 4:263–279

Burrough B, Helyar J (2004) Barbarians at the Gate: Fall of R.J.R. Nabisco, Random House, New York

Chaplinsky S, Niehaus G, Van de Gucht L (1998) Employee Buyouts: Causes, Structure, and Consequences, Journal of Financial Economics 48:283–332

Chapman JL, Klein PG (2009) Value Creation in Middle-Market Buyouts: A Transaction-Level Analysis. In: Cumming D (Ed) Companion to Private Equity – forthcoming, Wiley, New York

CMBOR (2001) Survey of the Economic and Social Impact of Management Buyouts & Buyins in Europe, EVCA Research Paper, Brussels

CMBOR (2004) Studie naar de economische en sociale effecten van buyouts in Nederland, NVP Research Paper, Amsterdam

CMBOR (2005) Private Equity and Generational Change – The Contribution of Private Equity to the Succession of Family Businesses in Europe, EVCA Research Paper, Brussels

CMBOR (2008) Economic and Social Effects of Buy-outs in the Netherlands, NVP Research Paper, Amsterdam

CMBOR/EVCA (2008) The Impact of Private Equity-backed Buyouts on Employee Relations, EVCA Research Paper, Brussels

Cressy R, Munari F, Malipiero A (2008) Creative Destruction? UK Evidence that Buyouts Cut Jobs to Raise Returns, Working Paper, University of Birmingham/University of Bologna, Birmingham/Bologna

Davis SJ, Haltiwanger J, Jarmin R, Lerner J, Miranda J (2008) Private Equity and Employment, Working Paper CES 08-07, Center for Economic Studies/U.S. Bureau of the Census, Washington

Deutsche Beteiligungs AG/FINANCE (2004) Economic Impact of Private Equity in Germany, FINANCE-Studies, Frankfurt

Ernst & Young (2007) How Do Private Equity Investors Create Value? A Study of 2006 Exits in the US and Western Europe, Ernst&Young Study, London

Faber O (2006) Finanzinvestoren in Deutschland – Portraits und Investitionsbeispiele, Arbeitspapier 123, Working Paper 123, Hans Böckler Stiftung, Düsseldorf

Fox I, Marcus A (1992) The Causes and Consequences of Leveraged Management Buyouts, Academy of Management Review 17(1):62–85

Hall D (2007) Methodological Issues in Estimating the Impact of Private Equity Buyouts on Employment, Working Paper, University of Greenwich, Greenwich

Hanney J (1986) The Management Buy-Out – An Offer You Can't Refuse!, OMEGA International Journal of Management Science 14(2):119–134

Harris R, Siegel DS, Wright M (2005) Assessing the Impact of Management Buyouts on Economic Efficiency: Plant-level Evidence from the United Kingdom, The Review of Economics and Statistics 87(1):148–153

Heinkel R, Zechner J (1990) The Role of Debt and Preferred Stock as a Solution to Adverse Investment Incentives, in: The Journal of Financial and Quantitative Analysis 25(1):1–24

Ippolito RA, James WA (1992) LBOs, Reversions and Implicit Contracts, Journal of Finance 47(1):139–166

Jensen MC (1986) Agency Costs of Free Cash Flow, Corporate Finance, and Takeovers, American Economic Review 76(2):323–329

Jensen MC (1989) Eclipse of the Public Corporation. In: Harvard Business Review 67:61–74

Kaplan SN (1989) The Effects of Management Buyouts on Operating Performance and Value, Journal of Financial Economics 24:217–254

Kaplan SN (1991) The Staying Power of Leveraged Buyouts, in: Journal of Financial Economics 29:287–313

Kaplan SN, Strömberg P (2008) Leveraged Buyouts and Private Equity, Working Paper, University of Chicago Graduate School of Business and NBER, Chicago

Lichtenberg FR, Siegel DS (1990) The Effects of Leveraged Buyouts on Productivity and Related Aspects of Firm Behaviour, Journal of Financial Economics 27:164–194

Liebeskind J, Wiersema M, Hansen G (1992) LBOs, Corporate Restructuring, and the Incentive-Intensity Hypothesis, Financial Management 21(1):73–88

Malone SC (1989) Characteristics of Smaller Company Leveraged Buyouts, Journal of Business Venturing, 4:349–359

Marti Pellon J, Alemany L, Zieling N, Salas de la Hera M (2005) Impact of VC & Private Equity in Spain: Period 1991–2002, ASCRI Research Paper, Madrid

Marti Pellon J, Alemany L, Zieling N, Salas de la Hera M (2007) Economic and Social Impact of Venture Capital & Private Equity in Spain 2007, ASCRI Research Paper, Madrid

Muscarella CJ, Vetsuypens MR (1990) Efficiency and Organizational Structure: A Study of Reverse LBOs, Journal of Finance 65(5):1389–1413

Opler T (1992) Operating Performance in Leveraged Buyouts: Evidence from 1985–1989, Financial Management 21(1):27–34

PSE (2007) Hedge Funds and Private Equity – A Critical Analysis, PSE Study, Brussels

PWC/AIFI (2006) Economic Impact of Private Equity and Venture Capital in Italy, PWC/AIFI Study, Milan

PWC/BVK (2005): Der Einfluss von Private-Equity Gesellschaften auf die Portfoliounternehmen und die deutsche Wirtschaft, PWC/BVK Study, Munich 2005

Rappaport A (1990) The Staying Power of the Public Corporation, Harvard Business Review 68(1):96–104

SEIU (2007) Behind the Buyouts – Inside the World of Private Equity, SEIU Study, Washington

Shapiro RJ, Pham ND (2008) American Jobs and the Impact of Private Equity Transactions, Private Equity Council, Washington

Shleifer A, Summers LH (1988) Breach of Trust in Hostile Takeovers. In: Auerbach AJ (Ed): From Corporate Takeovers: Causes and Consequences, UMI, Chicago, p 33–56

Smith AJ (1990) Corporate Ownership Structure and Performance, Journal of Financial Economics 27:143–164

Strömberg P (2008) The New Demography of Private Equity. In: World Economic Forum (Ed): Globalization of Alternative Investments Working Papers Volume 1 – The Global Economic Impact of Private Equity Report 2008, Cologny/Geneva, p 3–26

Taylor A, Bryant C (2007) Private Equity Deals that Cement Growth, Financial Times on 1 April 2007, p 7, London

Thompson S, Wright M (1995) Corporate Governance: The Role of Restructuring Transactions, Economic Journal 105 (May): 690–703

Toubeau V (2006) Private Equity Firms in Belgium – Value Creators or Locusts?, Working Paper – Unpublished Document, Solvay Business School, Brussels

Tranfield D, Denyer D, Smart P (2003) Towards a Methodology for Developing Evidence-Informed Management Knowledge by Means of Systematic Review, British Journal of Management 14:207–222

Weir C, Jones P, Wright M (2008) Public to Private Transactions, Private Equity and Performance in the UK: An Empirical Analysis of the Impact of Going Private, Working Paper, Robert Gordon University/Nottingham University, Aberdeen

Wright M, Chiplin B, Thompson S, Robbie K (1990) Management Buy-outs, Trade Unions and Employee Ownership, Industrial Relations Journal 21(2):136–146

Wright M, Coyne J, Lockley H (1984) Management Buyouts and Trade Unions: Dispelling the Myths, Industrial Relations Journal, 15(3):45–52

Wright M, Gilligan J, Amess K (2009) The Economic Impact of Private Equity: What We Know and What We Would Like to Know. In: Venture Capital: An International Journal of Entrepreneurial Finance 11(1):1–21

Wright M, Hoskisson RE, Busenitz LW (2001) Firm Rebirth: Buyouts as Facilitators of Strategic Growth and Entrepreneurship, Academy of Management Executive, 15(1):111–125

Wright M, Hoskisson RE, Busenitz LW, Dial J (2000) Entrepreneurial Growth Through Privatization: The Upside of Management Buyouts, Academy of Management Review 25(3):591–601

Wright M, Thompson S, Robbie K (1992) Venture Capital and Management-Led, Leveraged Buy-outs: A European Perspective, Journal of Business Venturing 7:47–71

Zahra SA (1995) Corporate Entrepreneurship and Financial Performance: The Case of Management Leveraged Buyouts, Journal of Business Venturing 10:225–247

Leichter lernen, effizienter studieren!

WWW.GABLER.D

Stickel-Wolf, Christine | Wolf, Joachim
Wissenschaftliches Arbeiten und Lerntechniken
Erfolgreich studieren – gewusst wie!
5., akt. u. überarb. Aufl. 2009. XVI, 384 S.
Mit 30 Abb. u. 19 Tab.
Br. EUR 29,90
ISBN 978-3-8349-0842-1

In diesem Buch finden Sie ausführliche Tipps zum rationellen, verhaltens- und behaltensorientierten Lesen, zum aktiven Zuhören und Mitschreiben, zum zielführenden Arbeiten in der Gruppe, zur Erstellung und Präsentation wissenschaftlicher Arbeiten, zur effizienten Vorbereitung auf Prüfungen und Klausuren sowie zur erfolgsgerichteten Studienplanung und -organisation. **Hotline: hilfe@bwl.uni-kiel.de**

Der Inhalt
- Effizientes Lesen und Zuhören
- Arbeiten in Gruppen
- Erstellung und Präsentation wissenschaftlicher Arbeiten
- Mündliche Wissenspräsentation
- Zielführende Prüfungsvorbereitung
- Studienplanung und -organisation

Die Autoren
Christine Stickel-Wolf ist Diplom-Pädagogin und freiberufliche Trainerin in Unternehmen und öffentlichen Einrichtungen.
Professor Dr. Joachim Wolf ist Inhaber des Lehrstuhls für Organisation der Christian-Albrechts-Universität zu Kiel.

Einfach bestellen:
kerstin.kuchta@gwv-fachverlage.de
Telefon +49(0)611. 7878-626

KOMPETENZ IN SACHEN WIRTSCHAFT

Antecedents of Style Drift in Private Equity Investments

Rainer Lauterbach, Isabell M. Welpe, Benjamin Langer

Abstract: Using a unique private equity fund dataset, we examine the antecedents of style drift in private equity investments. We find that fund size and investment amount are positively correlated with style drift and that investment fund experience is negatively associated with style drift. Our study complements the recent literature that examines the style drift question theoretically. Overall, our results hold implications for investment managers, portfolio companies and private equity investors.

Keywords: Style drift · Style investing · Co-movement · Private equity · Venture capital

JEL Classification: G24 · G11 · G32

Acknowledgements
We would like to thank the editors of this special issue as well as two anonymous reviewers, who contributed their comments, suggestions, and advice to our manuscript.

Dr. R. Lauterbach (✉)
Faculty of Economics and Business Administration, Johann Wolfgang Goethe-University, Mertonstr. 17, D-60325 Frankfurt am Main (Germany), Tel: (49) 170 340 1248, rlauterbach@alumni.upenn.edu

Prof. Dr. I. M. Welpe (✉)
Chair for Strategy and Organization, TUM Business School, Technical University of Munich, Leopoldstr. 139, D-80804 Munich (Germany), Tel: +49 (0)89 2023 8774, welpe@tum.de

Dipl.-Kfm. B. Langer (✉)
Faculty of Economics and Business Administration, Johann Wolfgang Goethe-University, Mertonstr. 17, D-60325 Frankfurt am Main (Germany), Tel: (49) 69 5480 5570, benjamin.langer@stud.uni-frankfurt.de

1 Introduction

Understanding the antecedents of mutual and private equity (PE) funds' change in investment focus ("style drift") is an important research issue (cf. Chan et al. 2002; Barberis/ Shleifer 2003; Black/McMillan 2004; Chen/De Bondt 2004; Pomorski 2004; Teo/Woo 2004; Cumming et al. 2005). Barberis and Shleifer (cf. Barberis/Shleifer 2003) coined the term "style investing" for funds following a certain strategy and according to several studies (cf. Barberis/Shleifer 2003; Teo/Woo 2004; Chen/De Bondt 2004), investors in the mutual fund industry classify risky assets into different investment styles and allocate capital to varying styles. "Style drift" occurs whenever funds pursue investments and finance companies that differ from their stated investment focus (cf. Barberis/Shleifer, 2003). To date the phenomena of style drift has mainly been studied in the mutual funds literature (cf. Brown/Goetzmann 1997; Brown/Goetzmann 2001; Taffler 1999), with Basu (cf. Basu 1977) and Banz (cf. Banz 1981) carrying out pioneering studies on portfolio investment according to firm characteristics. Brown and Van Harlow (cf. Brown/ Van Harlow 2004) argue that funds that have a consistent investment strategy earn positive returns in comparison to those that do not. Teo and Woo (cf. Teo/Woo 2004) study the effects of style investing in a cross-section sample of stock returns, whereas Fung and Hsieh (cf. Fung/Hsieh 2002), Bares et al. (cf. Bares et al. 2001) and Brown and Goetzmann (cf. Brown/Goetzmann 2001) study the implications of style investing and style consistency in the hedge fund industry.

Similarly to mutual funds, private equity funds (PEFs) usually describe themselves as being focused on a particular segment, in other words as following a particular "style". This focus may be on a specific industry, a geographic region or, most commonly, on a specific development stage[1] of financed companies (cf. Sahlman 1990; Gompers/Lerner 1999a). In this sense, many PEFs market themselves as being "early stage", "expansion", or "buy-out" funds in order for investors to assess where their capital will be invested. Institutional investors increasingly categorize their investments into asset classes to allow them to better assess and control their portfolio risk and to facilitate investments' comparison to standard benchmarks (cf. Chan et al. 2002; Barberis/Shleifer 2003; Brown/Van Harlow 2004; Avramov/Wermers 2006). To keep their portfolio balanced, investors pay special attention to a fund's stated stage focus. Consequently, the style and stage consistency of the PEFs' subsequent investment process is vital for institutional investors investing in those funds.

Style drift of private equity funds poses several potential risks for investors: First, it changes the fund's risk and return profile and therefore also the risk and return profile of the limited partner's invested capital. Even if style drifts result in successful investments, limited partners may not be willing to bear the increased overall fund risk implied inherent in such investments, especially if general partners "style drift" from later stages to earlier stages. Second, since some investors allocate an important share of their assets to private equity, the impact of changes within the limited partner's portfolio on the overall performance could be substantial[2]. Third, capital committed and provided to PEFs is very illiquid and investors may not be able to liquidate or rebalance their positions for many years. Investments in early stage companies may take more than 5 years to be sufficiently mature to sell, and several financing rounds may be required before an exit is possible (cf. Sahlman 1990). Given these risks for investors, style drift also poses a potential threat to private equity as an asset class; understanding its determinants and consequences is thus important (cf. Cumming et al. 2005).

Despite the relevance of style inconsistency and the related positive and negative consequences that such behavior may have in private markets, the phenomenon has to date received little to no attention in the private equity literature. The goal of this paper therefore is to introduce the concept of style drift in venture capital (VC) and private equity[3]. To shed some light on the antecedents of style drift, we pose the following research question: What are the determinants that lead PEFs to style drift their investments?

We analyzed investment styles and drift between styles in respect of private equity and venture capital investments analogous to the way that style drift in public equity has been studied. Generally, risky assets within PE and venture capital (VC) funds are categorized according to several factors, the most important being the region, industry, or the portfolio company's development stage (cf. Sahlman 1990). We focus this study on investment style with regard to the development stage of the portfolio company, as several studies confirm that this factor is an investment's key differentiating risk factor (cf. Brown/Goetzmann 1997; Teo/Woo 2004). We then derive hypotheses that link fund size, investment fund experience, and investment amount to the occurrence of style drift.

The general lack of substantial quantitative empirical studies regarding previous research on PEF performance is most likely due to the entire industry's *private* nature. While disclosure requirements force mutual funds to release information to the public (enabling their use for academic research), private equity companies are reluctant to disclose in-depth financial information. We test our hypotheses by using a unique international dataset of 426 investments spanning the period between 1986 and 2003.

The remainder of the paper is organized as follows: the next section develops hypotheses with regard to the antecedents of style drift. Following the data and methodology section, we provide the confirmatory results regarding style drift's key determinants. The concluding section presents a discussion and suggestions regarding areas of future research that would tie in with our results as well as with those in the PEF literature, and a discussion of our findings' implications for theory and practice.

2 Theory and hypotheses development

2.1 The determinants of style drift

In recent years, studies have paid increasing attention to PEF managers' investment behavior. There has been particular interest in the analysis of cash flows, private equity investments' return and risk characteristics, and these factors' consequences for valuations and investment decisions. No studies to date have looked at style drift in the Private Equity Industry in relation to the investment manager's behavior. The study of Gompers and Lerner (cf. Gompers/Lerner 2000) offers a potential explanation for why investment managers may be drifting by suggesting that when capital inflows into the private equity industry increase, valuations increase as a result of "too much money chasing too few deals". Similarly, Inderst and Müller (cf. Inderst/Müller 2004) suggest that overall market conditions affect the deal structure, entrepreneurs and PEFs' bargaining power and consequently, early stage companies' valuations. Ljungqvist and Richardson (cf. Ljungqvist/ Richardson 2003a, 2003b) provide the first notion of style drift's consequences for the private equity industry based on their analyses of the cash flow, return and risk characteristics of the Private Equity industry as well as of research on the investment behaviour of Private Equity fund managers. However, conclusions on style drift can only indirectly be derived from their studies as they do not directly analyze the phenomenon of style drift. Style drift is defined as a fund's initial investment into a portfolio company that belongs to a market-segment different from the fund's stated market segment focus. For example, if a venture capital fund has set its investment focus on early stage deals and does invest ten out of ten portfolio companies in the early stage VC market segment, then no style drift has occurred. However, if this fund would invest one initial investment into a pre-IPO-company, this would not fit within its stated investment focus and therefore would define one investment style drift. The antecedents of style drift have an impact on the number of drift transactions observed within the total dataset. In the following section, three antecedents of style drift are discussed in detail: the size of the Private Equity fund, the experience of the investment fund and the investment amount. All three factors influence the allocation decision and particularly style drift.

2.2 Fund size's influence on style drift

According to Kanniainen and Keuschnigg's (cf. Kanniainen/Keuschnigg 2003) optimal portfolio theory, there exists an optimal number of investments for every fund, since fund managers face a trade-off regarding the intensity of advice to their portfolio companies and overall portfolio size. To maintain or even to achieve the optimal number of portfolio companies during times of increased competition in a particular market segment, managers could consider attractive deals in other market segments rather than adding less attractive deals within their investment focus. This argument is in line with Barberis and Shleifer's (cf. Barberis/Shleifer 2003) style investing theory. An increase in fund size could increase the fund managers' incentives and flexibility to style drift due to their improved ability to afford due diligence and external advice's high costs. This would decrease the investment manager's need to rely on his own skills in a specific stage focus and lower the hurdle to switch to an adjacent stage. Previous studies, for example, Gompers and Lerner (cf. Gompers/Lerner 2000) have provided empirical evidence that increased competition, in their terms of 'money chasing deals', has an impact on increasing Private Equity valuations. Despite the fact that these authors have not gone a step further and analyzed, whether an increase in competition and valuation implies an effect on investment profitability, it is plausible to assume that it does. If increased competition implies lower profitability, then one should expect increased style drifts from those funds that can afford to style drift. Similarly, in this study, we focus on the impact of increased competition on the investment behaviour particularly on investment style drifts. Style drifts are associated with transaction costs due to investments in a different segments and transaction costs due to additional due diligences for the new investments in a new segment (cf. Cummings et al. 2005). We argue that it is plausible to assume that larger funds will simply be more able to bear the transaction costs involved with style drifting and thus more able to afford style.

Hypothesis 1: *Fund size is positively associated with style drift.*

2.3 Fund's experience's influence on style drift

As a proxy for experience, we measure a VC or PE fund management firm's number of quarters since its establishment until its initial investment into a portfolio company. Fund's experience plays a key role in attracting new deals as well as in raising capital, as confirmed, for example, by Cumming et al. (cf. Cummings et al. 2005). Funds with more years in business generally have a better reputation, a wider network from which to draw deal flow as well as better screening abilities within their segment. They consequently have better access to the most attractive deals within their investment focus and less incentive to drift their investment. Basically, when a fund management team has strong experience within a particular market segment, for example in start-up deals, it has become well connected with segment specific sources of deal flow, for example spin-offs of research institutions. More experience will foremost increase the network to segment specific sources of deal flow. Funds with long years of successful investment experience within their stage focus are less tempted towards potential deal flow in other stages than their original stage focus, because these experienced funds have optimized their skills and investment abilities within their original stage focus.

Hypothesis 2: *Fund's experience is negatively associated with style drift.*

2.4 Total investment amount's influence on style drift

In the context of this study we measure the investment amount with the total amount of cash inflows into a company from the initial investment tranche to the exit. In-line with Barberis and Shleifer's (cf. Barberis/Shleifer 2003) style investing theory, we postulate that fund managers will only drift from their specified investment focus, if a deal's expected relative performance in another segment is significantly higher. Moreover, fund managers are concerned about the overall risk of the portfolio and therefore would only drift, if the new investment opportunity has a lower expected risk than the average investment opportunity within the fund's stage focus. If an investment opportunity outside the fund's investment focus was found that increases the overall performance of the fund and does not increase the overall risk of the portfolio, then investment managers will allocate a higher amount of capital into that investment. By doing so, a manager can optimally invest the capital committed to the fund and at the same time concentrate its managerial resources on a reduced number of investments. In addition, deal valuations increase in periods of more intense competition as shown by Gompers and Lerner (cf. Gompers/Lerner 2000). That means that a fund has to invest more capital per deal during periods of increased competition and higher valuations in order to acquire the same level of equity, influence and profit share of its portfolio company. In line with previous explanations it can be expected that funds show investment style drifts foremost during periods of increased competition, which are also the periods of increased valuations leading to deals with increased investment volumes. Consequently, it can be expected that investment amount is positively associated with style drift.

Hypothesis 3: *Investment amount is positively associated with style drift.*

3 Methodology

We merged the Venture Economics (www.thomsonfinancial.com) data – which is very comprehensive in respect of each financing round but does not contain information about each round's separate cash flow tranches – with the CEPRES database (www.cepres.de) data – which provides details on each cash transaction and whose information is based on due diligence and monitoring reports, partially including investment firms' audited filings. The Venture Economics database has been used for empirical studies on the private equity industry a number of times over the last decade (cf. Lerner, 1994a; 1994b).

The CEPRES dataset is somewhat related to other VC and entrepreneurial finance papers with cross-country datasets. The scope of our data is similar to Black and Gilson (cf. Black/Gilson 1998) and Jeng and Wells (cf. Jeng/Wells 2000), but those datasets are based on aggregate industry figures and do not contain transaction-specific information. Our dataset allows a detailed analysis of investment style. By merging the Venture Economics and CEPRES databases' comprehensive information, we increase the validity of our analyses and are able to study more than 150 original variables in respect of each investment, thus making a very detailed analysis of both datasets' intersection possible. At the time of the merger of the two databases in November 2003, CEPRES contained 5,308 investments into 4,476 portfolio companies provided by 229 funds belonging to 74 fund management firms. The data obtained from Venture Economics includes 178,300 financing rounds. The entries of the two datasets are matched on four different levels: the name of the fund management firm, the name of the fund, the name of the portfolio company and the date of the fund's initial investment in the portfolio company. The matching resulted in 1,774 investments with congruent entries on all four levels in both databases. To avoid reporting bias potentially inherent in unrealized investments, the dataset was reduced to 1,011 cases of fully and partially realized investments. Since our study was focuses on investment style, we further consider only those investments with complete information on the specific investment focus at all three levels: the management firm, the fund, and the company. To identify drifts in investment style, funds or management firms with a general focus[4] were also removed from the sample, as an investment drift would not be defined in respect of these cases. To avoid a double count, we then also removed the cases where the same investment management firm's follow-on fund invested in a company already considered in respect of the predecessor fund.

After the merger of the databases and the above-mentioned adjustments of the sample for the style drift analyses, our dataset encompasses 426 investments made in 411 portfolio companies by 63 different venture capital and PEFs belonging to 29 investment management firms. These investments include 763 financing rounds and 1,118 cash transactions between June 1986 and March 2003. During this period of more than 15 years, the venture capital and private equity industry went through different cycles, including the Internet bubble period between roughly September 1998 and March 2000. Therefore, no significant loss of generality arose from the shortening of the dataset. We consider the dataset to be representative with regard to the frequency distribution of the investments, showing a steady increase from 1995 onward and a peak during 1998 and 1999, where 38.03% of all observations are concentrated. The number of financings in the sample drops after the Internet bubble burst in 2000: only 26 observations (6.10% of the sample) fall in the period after the crash. This sample thus matches generally the market's investment behavior pattern during the entire period.

The country distribution of this dataset is also similar to the respective proportions of the market sizes: the majority of the investments (239), representing 66.9% of the sample, were carried out in the USA, which continues to be the most significant private equity market. 114 investments were made in Europe (31.9%), with the UK, France and Germany being the biggest markets with 51, 35 and 17 investments respectively. No country was specified with regard to 69 investments (16.2%). As far as the focus of our study is concerned, the distribution of the portfolio companies' development stages is as follows:

Table 1. Absolute and Relative Frequency of Drift by Venture Capital and PEFs
This table presents the frequencies of stage drifts by private equity limited partnerships between 1986 and 2003. In total, 205 investments out of the complete sample of 426 investments have been drifted. We have classified the stage preferences of private equity investment management firms and portfolio companies into six categories, which are listed for the investment managers in the second row as well as for the portfolio companies in the second column. The upper table gives the frequencies of stage drift in absolute terms while the bottom one gives them in per cent terms. The analysis included only funds of those investment management firms, for which the databases Venture Economics or CEPRES stated a specific stage investment focus. Thus investment management firms defined as "generalists" are not included in this analysis, as a stage drift can not be defined for such funds. The matrix of column 3 to 8 and row 3 to 8 pairs for each cell the number of portfolio companies at financed by investment managers out of their stated stage focus. For example: in nineteen cases, investment managers with a focus on early stage deals provided their initial financing to companies at the expansion stage. Column 9 provides the total number of portfolio companies having received their initial financing from investment management firms through style drift. Row 9 gives the total number of drifts by investment management firms for the different focuses.

		Investment Manager Stage Preference						
		Seed	Early	Expansion	Later	Mezzanine	Buyout	Total
Stage of Portfolio Company	Seed	0	11	0	0	0	0	11
	Early	0	0	0	0	0	0	0
	Expansion	0	19	0	0	33	0	52
	Later	0	12	27	0	1	3	43
	Mezzanine	0	1	0	0	0	0	1
	Buyout	0	2	0	0	96	0	98
	Total	0	45	27	0	130	3	205
		Investment Manager Stage Preference						
		Seed	Early	Expansion	Later	Mezzanine	Buyout	Total
Stage of Portfolio Company	Seed	0.0%	24.4%	0.0%	0.0%	0.0%	0.0%	5.4%
	Early	0.0%	0%	0.0%	0.0%	0.0%	0.0%	0.0%
	Expansion	0.0%	42.2%	0.0%	0.0%	25.4%	0.0%	25.4%
	Later	0.0%	26.7%	100%	0.0%	0.8%	100%	210%
	Mezzanine	0.0%	2.2%	0.0%	0.0%	0.0%	0.0%	0.5%
	Buyout	0.0%	4.4%	0.0%	0.0%	73.8%	0.0%	47.8%
	Total	0.0%	100%	100%	0.0%	100%	100%	100%

leveraged buy-outs (34.7%), mezzanine (3.9%), later stage (9.2%), expansion stage (12.2%), early stage (33.1%) and seed stage (70%). In 235 cases (55.2% of the sample), the investments were made by venture capital funds, in 143 cases (33.6%) by mezzanine funds, and in 48 cases (11.3%) by buy-out funds. In terms of industry sector, most investments are related to either the Health Care and Life Science or the information technology sectors (14% each) followed by the Industrial/Manufacturing sector with 53 investments (12.8%), Software and Telecommunications, both with 43 investments (1.4% each), Internet 23 (5.6%), Consumer Diversified 19 (4.6%), Retail 16 (3.9%), Semiconductors 11 (2.6%), Media and Financial Services with 8 each (1.9%), Materials with 7 (1.7%), and other industries with 67 investments (16.2%). No sector could be specified in respect of only 12 investments.

Table 1 presents the frequencies of stage drifts by private equity limited partnerships between 1986 and 2003. In total, 205 investments out of the complete sample of 426 investments have been drifted.

The illustration in table 1 shows a total of 205 drifted investments, of which only 3 belong to investment funds with a buy-out stage preference. This small number emphasizes that buy-out funds have a lesser tendency to drift. One reason could be that the buy-out investment market could have offered extraordinary attractive investment conditions, which might have hindered the buy-out funds to drift into other segments. This also could contribute to the fact that investment funds with original stage preferences other than buy-out drifted intensively into the buy-out market segment, including 98 drifts, which are 48% of all observed drifts.

4 Variable definitions and summary statistics

4.1 Dependent variables

4.1.1 Style drift

According to Barberis and Shleifer (cf. Barberis/Shleifer 2003): "To test any predictions that emerge from a model of style investing, it is important to have a concrete way of identifying styles". In the mutual fund industry, investors classify risky assets into different styles and allocate capital to varying styles (cf. Chen/De Bondt 2004; Teo/Woo 2004). We analyze investment styles and drift between styles in respect of private equity and venture capital investments analogous to public equity's style concept. Generally, risky assets within PE and VC funds are categorized according to several factors, primarily by the portfolio company's region, industry, or development stage. Sahlman (cf. Sahlman 1990) and others have observed that venture capital and PEFs focus their investment strategy on different stages of the portfolio company's development. This strategy focus can be interpreted as a particular investment style. VC and PE funds are therefore able to style drift between different stages. We thus focus this study on investment style with regard to development stage, as several studies confirm this factor as an investment's key differentiating risk factor. Plummer (cf. Plummer 1987) and Sahlman (cf. Sahlman 1990) describe the development stages' details, their underlying risks and fund managers' specific skill requirements.

Venture capital and private equity management firms pool investment managers with a superior expertise, skill set, and network within a *specific investment focus*, and base their investment style and strategy on this competitive advantage (cf. Wright/Robbie 1998). We classify fund management firms' focus into six different categories (Firm $_f$), with f being either "seed", "early stage", "expansion", "later stage", "mezzanine", or "buy-out". As fund managers raise funds with a limited partnership structure as well as a restricted lifetime, fund volume and investment focus, we also distinguish between three different investment fund strategies (Fund $_s$), where s stands for "venture capital", "mezzanine", or "buy-out" (cf. Wright/Robbie 1998). We furthermore maintain that venture capital includes the development stages "seed", "early stage", "expansion", and "later stage".

As a fund can provide its initial injection of capital into a portfolio company at different stages of the company's development (cf. Bigus 2006), we distinguish between six different development stages (Company $_{ds}$). The denomination of the development stages of the portfolio companies are the same as the denomination of the different styles for the fund management firm (Firm $_f$) mentioned above Based on the overlap of the categories Firm $_f$, Fund $_s$, and Company $_{ds}$, we define style drift as follows: *an investment style drift occurs when* a) the focus of investment management firm $_f$ does not equal the development stage of portfolio company $_{ds}$, and b) the strategy of fund $_s$ does not fit the development stage of portfolio company $_{ds}$. A brief summary of the respective development stages is given below.

Seed investments: Seed investments are associated with the highest risk, as they have to prove their concept or technology, gain a first customer as well as penetrate the market and find an exit. Information asymmetries between investors and entrepreneurs are highest at this stage, mainly due to a lack of tangible assets. The upside potential of seed investments is particularly high, as entry valuations tend to be very low and the business is fully scalable. Investors focusing on the seed stage usually need in-depth technical expertise and talent to guide the company through the first steps of development.

Early stage investments: In this study, early stage investments are considered a company's start-up and early development. The specific risks of this stage are building up a management team and developing the product's marketability.

Expansion investments: A company in the expansion stage faces the challenge of scaling up sales and market penetration. Risks involved are the rapid gain of market share, the establishment of brand recognition and, ideally, market leadership. Investors need to support a long-term growth strategy and offer business development know-how.

Later stage investments: Later stage investments also include profitable companies with poor cash flows as well as companies with growing rapidly towards the point of liquidity. Specific risks at this stage are, for example, the provision of working capital for the further expansion of manufacturing facilities, expanded marketing, and product enhancements. Fund managers focusing on this stage require strong ties to investment bankers, need to advise the company with regard to its preparation for exiting, and negotiate with potential buyers.

Mezzanine investments: Mezzanine financings are offered to companies with a certain level of stable cash flows or tangible assets. Risks include the business's stability, thus investors need skills to assess the company's financial structure and outlook.

Buyout investments: Buy-out investments involve a strategy in which a company, or a controlling stake of it, is acquired by using borrowed money (bonds or loans) to leverage the equity stake. The key risk associated with buy-out investments is the credit risk faced by financings with a high level of leverage, and a company development that is less good than expected. Investors need expertise in financial modeling and credit risk assessment.

PEFs usually cover the mezzanine and buy-out stages, whereas by venture capital funds usually cover the remaining stages.

4.2 Independent variables

4.2.1 Fund size

We measure fund size as the total amount of capital committed to a specific fund.

4.2.2 Fund experience

As a proxy for experience, we measure a VC or PE fund management firm's number of quarters between its establishment and the initial investment in the relevant portfolio company.

4.2.3 Investment amount

This variable measures the total amount of cash inflows into a company from the initial investment tranche to the exit.

We also use a number of control variables regarding market conditions, characteristics of the fund management as well as characteristics of the portfolio company in our analyses. Specifically we control (1) on the level of market conditions for the number of private equity backed IPOs during the year of the observed investment as an indicator for exit activities in the market and for the risk free rate of US government bonds as an indicator for the market interest during the investment period, (2) on the level of fund characteristics for the number of years between the fund's final closing and the fund's initial investment into the observed portfolio company as an indicator for the fund's maturity and (3) on the level of the portfolio company whether it is a high-tech-related deal as an indicator for increased technology risk.

5 Results

Our empirical analysis consists of three steps. We first present binary logistic regression estimates relating to the determinants of style drift, including various control variables. Thereafter, we use ordinary least squares regressions in a "log-log" framework to determine the independent variables' influence on the investment's performance.

5.1 The occurrence of style drift

205 (48.1% of the sample) of the 426 investments in the sample were style drifted. Style drifts are therefore quite common and a detailed analysis of style drift's determinants and impact is important for a better understanding of the venture capital and private equity industry. Mezzanine funds are the most likely to style drift their investments (130 cases), accounting for 63.11% of all observed drifts, most of which occurred by financing buy-out transactions (96). Early stage funds account for more than 20% of drifts. However, there were no style drifts by venture capital funds specializing in seed and later stage investments, or by buy-out funds. An explanation for this could be that seed and buy-outs investments represent both ends of the private equity investment chain and thus require a higher grade of specialization. As the information asymmetries and risks are highest in seed investments, investors focusing on this stage need very specialized expertise more than any other venture capitalist. Only 11 investments were drifted to seed companies. Furthermore, these drifts were led by early stage funds, so the differences in the adjacent investment focus may not be as significant as those in the more distinct stages. Style drifts to buy-out investments were the most common ones (99 investments) representing around 48.06% of all drifts. Almost all drifts to the buy-out stage, with two notable exceptions from early stage funds, were led by mezzanine funds. This again confirms that drifts occur mostly among style closely related to each other, as the underlying risks and the required management skills are more similar.

5.2 Results of the determinants of style drift

We examine the variables governing the relation between an observed stage drift in the full sample of 426 investments by means of binary logistic regression to shed light on the determinants of stage drift. We employ this method because our dependent variable "stage drift" is dichotomous in nature. In our regression analysis, we control for market environment, time of investment, fund characteristics and portfolio firm characteristics to isolate the effects of our main variables on the decision to drift an investment. The results of the regression models on the determinants of style drift are shown in table 2. An examination of table 2 reveals the results of the tests of hypotheses 1-3.

The results are very robust across all specifications and capture a fairly good amount of the variability of fund managers' style drift probability (pseudo-R^2 between 22.6% and 25.3%). The dependent variable is always a dummy equal to one for drifted investments, and zero for non-drifted investments. Our first hypothesis is confirmed by our analysis. There is a positive relation between the size of the fund and style drifts ($\beta = .006$ in model (2); $p < .001$). Regarding our second hypothesis, the results confirm that funds with increased experience are able to screen good business opportunities more successfully and may have built an extensive network to generate a steady deal-flow. The variable Investment Fund Experience does indeed negatively affect the probability of style drift ($\beta = -.581$ in model (2); $t < .01$). Finally, the variable Investment Amount positively affects the probability of style drift ($\beta = 1.21\text{E-}05$ in model (3); $t < .01$), which confirms hypothesis 3.

Table 2. Regression Analysis on the Determinants of Stage Drifts
The table presents a binary logistic regression analysis of the determinants of a stage drift by private equity funds. The sample consists of 426 investments made between 1986 and 2003 in 411 portfolio companies worldwide. A stage drift is defined as an investment management firm investing in a portfolio company which development stage at time of investments differs from the stated stage investment focus of the investment management firm. The dependent variable is a dummy variable with a value of 1 in case of a stage drift and a value of 0 otherwise. Stage drifts are regressed on the logarithm of the independent variables. Independent variables include a dummy variable controlling for investments during the internet bubble period, committed capital to the industry at time of investment and one period before investment, the risk free rate of US government bonds, the number of private equity backed IPOs during the year of the observed investment, and the change of the NASDAQ index during the three quarters before the investment and the total amount of capital committed to new private equity funds in the year of the observed investment. Fund characteristics are controlled for by the variables fund size, the number of years an investment management firm has been active in the private equity industry and the years between the fund's final closing and the fund's initial investment into the observed portfolio company. Variables to control for company characteristics include the total amount invested into the company from all investors accumulated over the company's lifetime and the age of the company at time of the observed investment. A competition variable indicating the number of new private equity funds raised during the year of the observed investment is also included. The table presents the results for 6 different regression models to test the robustness of coefficients. For all variables, the coefficients and significance level is given. The model parameters include the number of observations, the pseudo-R^2 and the X^2 statistics for all regression with the associated p-value.

		Model (1)	Model (2)	Model (3)	Model (4)	Model (5)	Model (6)
		Dependent Variable = Investment drift	Dependent Variable = Investment drift	Dependent Variable = Investment drift	Dependent Variable = Investment drift	Dependent Variable = Investment drift	Dependent Variable = Investment drift
	Constant	0.259	-2.120 *	0.216	-0.507	0.763	0.045
H1: Fund Size		0.004 **	0.006 ***	0.004 ***	0.005 ***	0.004 **	0.005 ***
H2: Investment Fund Experience		-0.480 ***	-0.581 ***	-0.479 ***	-0.534 ***	-0.453 ***	-0.513 ***
H3: Investment Amount		9.49 E-05**	7.87 E-05**	1.21 E-04***	9.96 E-04 ***	1.04 E-04 ***	9.55 E-04 ***
Age of company		0.014	0.017				
Time to Invest		0.153	0.179	0.238 **	0.223 **		
Investment in Bubble				0.169	0.342		
No. of IPOs				2.85 E-04	-6.13E-04	0.001	4.41E-04
Risk Free Rate		-0.052	-0.041	-0.058	-0.021	-0.112	-0.090
NASDAQ Development		-1.284 *	-2.480 ***	-1.585 **	-1.685 **	-1.616 **	-1.724 **
Committed Capital		5.05E-06 **		4.80E-06 **		4.58E-06 **	
Competition [log]			0.805 ***		0.344 *		0.354 *
No. of Observations		248	248	308	308	308	308
Pseudo R^2		0.234	0.253	0.245	0.237	0.234	0.226
X^2		66.043	72.361	86.585	83.441	82.041	78.902
p-value		0.000	0.000	0.000	0.000	0.000	0.000

6 Discussion and Conclusion

We set out to understand the reasons behind funds drifting on their investments. We considered both market and fund characteristics as antecedents of style drift. The results have theoretical and practical implications for investment strategies in general and the private equity industry in particular.

In line with hypothesis 1, we furthermore find fund size to have a positive effect on stage drifts. According to our findings, an increase of USD 1 million in the size of the fund would lead to an increase of .5% in the probability of investment drift. This result is economically significant as the size of the median fund in our sample is USD 145.2 million and that of the average fund USD 181.8 million, thus the average fund in our sample was associated with an 18.3% greater probability of drifting investments than our median fund was. All of the above confirm that larger funds may be more prone to style drift.

Our results also confirm our second hypothesis. Funds with more experience do not seem to be prone to style drift. These findings support the argument that a more experienced investment fund has over the years built up an extensive network, a steady generation of deal flows, an increased expertise in the specific investment focus, and a reputation through its good track record. Reputation is important for fund managers as it enables them to access equity and debt markets (cf. Diamond 1989). This makes it easier for them to identify the best investment opportunities within a specific segment and gives them less incentive to switch to another market segment. In particular, doubling fund managers' time in business leads to a 58.1% reduction in the probability of style drift according to regression model (2). This result indicates that a larger proportion of less experienced funds tend to drift investments. This finding is in line with Gompers's (1996) grandstanding argument that younger firms seek to gain reputation rapidly. To raise follow-on funds quicker, younger firms are willing to move their investments towards an IPO faster, which could indicate that they are also more willing to drift their style to later stages.

Surprisingly, the mere .29 correlation between time in business and fund size suggests that fund size should not be used as a proxy for experience. Investment management firms specializing for example on early stage investments gain more experience as they raise and close funds but keep their fund size relatively constant to optimally invest the capital committed.

The total amount invested in a portfolio company has a positive effect on stage drifts. This result confirms our third hypothesis. In our regression analysis we find that an increase of USD 1 Mio. in the total amount invested is associated with an increased probability of stage drift of .01% according to regression model (3).

This paper is one of the first to examine the antecedents of style drift in private equity. This study adds to the existing literature in several respects. It primarily complements the recent analysis of style drift in private equity by Cumming et al. (cf. Cumming et al. 2005): we affirm the importance of understanding style drift in private equity by providing evidence of its substantial occurrence as predicted by Barberis and Shleifer's (cf. Barberis/Shleifer 2003) style-investing hypothesis. Furthermore, we confront the methodological limitations of the self-reported data inherent to the Venture Economics database that Cumming et al. (cf. Cumming et al. 2005) used by using a unique database that merges the Venture Economics database with the CEPRES database containing partially audited information.

The findings of this study indicate that PE funds state specific investment styles, but do not always invest within these stated limits. Typically, PE fund managers do not ask their fund investors prior to each deal for their permission to invest beyond their stated limits. This can lead to information asymmetries between the fund investors and the fund managers. The hazard of opportunistic behaviour in terms of ad hoc shifts in investment style is of relevance due to uncertainty in diversification. For example, if a fund investor wants to diversify his assets in two different funds according to their two different investment styles, but in practice one fund shows style drift so that in the end both funds focus on the same style, then the fund investor is "fooled" with an undiversified portfolio. Due to the intransparencies of the PE fund industry, the scope for and hazard of these ad hoc shifts cannot precisely be estimated, but is certainly important enough to be considered by any PE fund investor. Investors in PE funds have several options to address the risks of style drifts. Before their investment into a PE fund, they can include style drift related questions into the due diligence process to the fund management firm, for example: "What is the key focus of industry, region, development stage and other aspects of your anticipated portfolio companies? What is your process when you receive an attractive investment offer out of this stated focus and how will you inform the fund investors about this investment option? How do you resolve conflict of interests between your stated investment focus and investment proposals out of this focus (style drift)?" A fund investor can ask the fund management to integrate clear rules into the investment contract (private placement memorandum and limited partnership agreement) on how to deal with style drifts. One practical solution for this type of conflict of interest would be to allocate a board of advisors responsible to decide upon each portfolio investment outside of the fund's stated focus. After a fund investor has committed capital to a fund, the investor can monitor the fund manager's behaviour for example with style-drift specific questions and comments during annual meetings. In case the fund operates out of the originally agreed lines of operations and investment focus, the fund investor has legal ways for intervention and can refuse to inject further capital into the fund.

Our study also complements the recent literature that examines the style drift question theoretically. E.g. Barberis and Shleifer (cf. Barberis/Shleifer 2003) argue that certain styles' higher relative returns lead to money chasing styles in cycles of positive feedback trading. They further suggest that of assets within the same style will move more than their fundamentals, while the prices of assets in other styles will move less than their fundamentals.

On the investor level, commitment is guaranteed for the fund's total lifetime without the option to simply terminate the commitment and change to another fund in case of poor performance. On the fund manager level, his investment style has to follow the agreed upon focus. Further, an investment in a PE or VC portfolio company is generally not liquid, and poorly performing companies cannot simply be sold and traded for better performing deals. Due diligences and negotiation efforts incur high transaction costs for PE and VC investments. Consequently, the only way to drift the investment style within the fund's lifetime without generating high transaction costs is an investment in a new portfolio company that falls outside the fund's stated investment focus.

Our findings hold implications for investment managers, portfolio companies and private equity investors. One implication is that PE fund managers show opportunistic behavior beyond the level of their originally stated fund investment style limitations. This behavior could lead to an increased level of risk out of the range originally agreed upon by the fund's investor. This could be an opportunism issue, which is pertinent also in other fields in the corporate finance and financial intermediation literature. Another implication of the study of style drift is the analysis of contract design, penalty and incentive setting between the fund's investors and the fund's management team. In line with the current discussion of more transparency and control of the financial industry overall, the implications of this study could lead fund investors to requirements of more transparency and control in regards to the fund's investment style. For investment managers, our results suggest that it may be as important to understand the style that will be preferred by other investment managers at the time of the exit as providing non-financial value added to portfolio companies. The fund management could have several potential advantages to deviate from the initially communicated investment focus at the time when the fund was launched. Advantages in line with the interests of the fund investors are increased return on investments leading to higher income due to profit sharing incentives. Advantages in conflict of interest to the fund investors could be for example window dressing purposes helping the fund management to attract future fund investors but not helping current investors to increase returns.

For investors into PEF, our results are an indication that the originally targeted portfolio diversification before the fund's investment period is difficult to maintain during their investment period, since approximately half of PEFs exhibit style drift over the course of a fund's lifetime. Since style drift in private equity is associated with much higher transaction costs in terms of time and money invested, investors and investment managers may want to incorporate style calculation information into their investment strategies. Unlike public equity, private equity investments are harder to rebalance and transaction fees are much higher. Due to style drift's time intensity in private equity, it is associated with high opportunity costs for investment managers.

Future research may build on our findings in a number of ways. First, our results contradict authors, such as Brown and Harlow (cf. Brown/Harlow 2002), who find that style consistency is associated with higher results in public equity markets. Future studies might therefore want to examine the relation between style drift and performance. Second, future studies could examine whether investment managers' previous returns influence performance. Third, it would be interesting to examine whether previous returns in a particular stage lead to increased drifting of funds to that stage. Fourth, it would be a further field of research, whether changes of the level of committed capital into funds focusing on specific stages influences stage drifts to a particular stage. Another interesting question would be whether economic growth induces investment managers to leave public equity markets and to transfer their style drift practice to a private equity environment. Fifth, future research might focus on possible additional influencing factors beyond the antecedents of style drift analyzed in this study. Examples of other possible influencing factors could be changes in regional or industrial market segments for example like the bubble and burst of the Internet investment area between 1998 and 2001. Further factors could be changes in regulatory frameworks, which drive for example the health care and renewable industry sectors. This paper focuses on the occurrence of style drift and the key factors having an impact on this occurrence. In a future study it could be interesting to examine not only the number of style drifts, but also the size of the investments with style drift and in comparison the size of the other deals of an investment fund.

Furthermore, this study has focused on the number of style drifts. Future studies might build on this research by examining the role and prevalence of the volume of style drifts across different private equity segments.

Moreover, cognitive factors (e.g. pro-activeness of fund managers; risk-taking behaviour etc.) or external environmental factors may also play a role for the style drifting of investment managers. With regard to the latter it may be that economic conditions or changes in capital markets lead to a lack of investment opportunities, e.g. in specific industry sectors or development stages, which might prompt higher degrees of style drift. This may be, e.g., because fund management needs to look for alternative investment opportunities outside the fund's original investment focus (beyond the argument of "too much money chasing too few deals" concerning company valuation and potential returns on PE investments – and those arguments discussed by Barberis and Shleifer (cf. Barberis/ Shleifer 2003). This evasion or switching behaviour may be in particular for high-volume funds with a lot of "money to be put to work"; thus adding to the possible explanations for the relevance of fund size in influencing style shifts. Finally, our study is done at an investment level. Effects of style drift at fund level could deliver a more in-depth knowledge of fund managers' motives for drifting.

Endnotes

1 The classification of the specific development stages of a company is done according to the definitions and descriptions provided by Sahlman (cf. Sahlman 1990). The variable definitions in section 4 relate to the studies of Plummer (cf. Plummer 1987) and Sahlman (cf. Sahlman 1990), which describe the development stages' details, their underlying risks and fund managers' specific skill requirements. Typically, company developments can be characterized by different stages, which are introduced in detail by Sahlman (cf. Sahlman 1990). Private Equity and Venture Capital funds have specialized on these different development stages and state their investment style accordingly. Therefore, a Venture Capital fund stating "early stage focus" as its investment style invests in companies during their early stage of development. The term "later stage" congruently is related to the later "development stage" of a company.
2 For example, the Yale endowment, one of the largest endowments in the US with over $12 billion in assets under management, allocates more than 15% of their portfolio to private equity (Yale Endowment Report, 2004).
3 Following Cumming et al. (2005), we hereafter simply use the term "private equity". The distinction between private equity and the term venture capital is particularly blurred by the fact that VC funds often style drift into later stage investments – commonly referred to as "private equity" investments – and that PEFs likewise often style drift into earlier stage investments – commonly referred to as "venture capital" investments. For expositional simplicity, we therefore use private equity as the most generic term to refer to early stage venture capital as well as late stage private equity (Cumming et al., 2005).
4 A Private Equity fund that is stating "general focus" cannot be allocated to one single investment style. For example, only a fund that does explicitly state "early stage" as its investment focus is considered within its investment style when investing into an early stage company. If that fund would invest into a later stage deal that would counted as style drift. A fund stating "general focus" has a focus on more than one specific investment style.

References

Acs Z, Audretsch D (1994) New Firm Start-ups, Technology, and Macroeconomic Fluctuations, Small Business Economics 6:439–449
Avramov D, Wermers R (2006) Investing in Mutual Funds when Returns are Predictable, Journal of Financial Economics 81:339–377
Banz R (1981) The Relationship between Return and Market Value of Common Stocks, Journal of Financial Economics, 9:3–18
Barberis N, Shleifer A (2003) Style Investing. Journal of Financial Economics 68:161–199
Bares P, Gibson R, Gyger S (2001) Style Consistency and Survival Probability in the Hedge Funds Industry (EFA 2001 Barcelona Meetings, EFMA 2001 Lugano Meetings)
Basu S (1977) Investment Performance of Common Stocks in Relation to their Price Earnings Ratios: a Test of the Efficient Market Hypothesis, Journal of Finance 32:663–682
Bigus J (2006) Staging of Venture Financing, Investor Opportunism and Patent Law, Journal of Business Finance and Accounting 33:939–960
Birch R (1995) Managing Equity Style Exposure: a Plan Sponsor's Experience. In: Klein R, Lederman J (eds), Equity Style Management. (Irwin) pp 421–432
Black B, Gilson R (1998) Venture Capital and the Structure of Capital Markets: Banks versus Stock Markets. Journal of Financial Economics 46:243–277
Black AJ, McMillan DG (2004) Non-linear Predictability of Value and Growth Stocks and Economic Activity, Journal of Business Finance and Accounting 31:439–471
Brown K, Harlow W (2002) Staying the Course: the Impact of Investment Style Consistency on Mutual Fund Performance, Working P (University of Texas). Available at SSRN: http://ssrn.com/abstract=306999
Brown S, Goetzmann W (1997) Mutual Fund Styles, Journal of Financial Economics 43:373–399
Brown S, Goetzmann W (2001) Hedge Funds with Style, Working Paper (Yale University), EFA 2001 Barcelona Meetings. Available at SSRN: http://ssrn.com/abstract=261068
Chan L, Chen H, Lakonishok J (2002) On Mutual Fund Investment Styles, Review of Financial Studies 15:1407–1437
Chen H, De Bondt W (2004) Style Momentum within the S&P 500 Index, Journal of Empirical Finance 11:483–507
Cumming D, Fleming G, Schwienbacher A (2005) Style Drift in Private Equity, Working Paper. (University of Alberta and Australian National University). Available at SSRN: http://ssrn.com/abstract=729684
Diamond D (1989) Reputation Acquisition in Debt Markets, Journal of Political Economy 97:828–862
Florou A (2005) Discussion of Performance of Private to Public MBOs: The Role of Venture Capital, Journal of Business Finance and Accounting 32:683–690
Fung W, Hsieh D (2002) Asset-based Style Factors for Hedge Funds, Financial Analysts Journal 58:16–27
Gompers P (1996) Grandstanding in the Venture Capital Industry, Journal of Financial Economics 42:132–157
Gompers P, Lerner J (1996) The Use of Covenants: an Empirical Analysis of Venture Partnership Agreements, Journal of Law & Economics 39:463–498
Gompers P, Lerner J (1999a) The Venture Capital Cycle, MIT Press, Cambridge, MA
Gompers P, Lerner J (1999b) What Drives Venture Capital Fundraising?, Working Paper (Harvard Business School)
Gompers P, Lerner J (2000) Money Chasing Deals? The Impact of Fund Inflows on Private Equity Valuations, Journal of Financial Economics 55:281–324
Inderst R, Mueller H (2004) The Effect of Capital Market Characteristics on the Value of Start-up Firms, Journal of Financial Economics 72:319–356
Jeng L, Wells P (2000) The Determinants of Venture Capital Funding: Evidence across Countries, Journal of Corporate Finance 6:241–289
Kanniainen V, Keuschnigg C (2003) The optimal Portfolio of Start-up Firms in Venture Capital Finance, Journal of Corporate Finance 9:521–534
Kaplan S, Schoar A (2005) Private Equity Performance: Returns, Persistence and Capital Flow, Journal of Finance 60:1791–1823
Lerner J (1994a) The Syndication of Venture Capital Investments, Financial Management 23:16–28
Lerner J (1994b) Venture Capitalists and the Decision to Go Public, Journal of Financial Economics 35:293–317
Ljungqvist A, Richardson M (2003a) The Cash Flow, Return and Risk Characteristics of Private Equity, Working Paper (MIT)

Ljungqvist A, Richardson M (2003b) The Investment Behaviour of PEF Managers, working Paper (London School of Economics)

Plummer J (1987) QED Report on Venture Capital Financial Analysis, QED Research, Palo Alto

Pomorski L (2004) Style Investing: Evidence from Mutual Funds, Working Paper (EFA 2004 Maastricht Meetings Paper No. 1163)

Sahlman W (1990) The Structure and Governance of Venture-capital Organizations, Journal of Financial Economics 27:473–522

Taffler R (1999) Discussion of the Profitability of Momentum Investing, Journal of Business Finance and Accounting 26:1093–1102

Teo M, Woo S-J (2004) Style Effects in the Cross-section of Stock Returns, Journal of Financial Economics 74:367–398

Yale Endowement Report (2004) Available at: www.yale.edu/about/Endowment_Update.pdf

Wright M, Robbie K (1998) Venture Capital and Private Equity: a Review and Synthesis, Journal of Business Finance and Accounting 25:521–570

Financing Young Biotechnology Companies: Public Support and Venture Capital in Comparison

Oliver Heneric, Peter Witt

Abstract: Due to long product development times, asset intense R&D processes, and high failure rates, young biotechnology firms frequently require huge amounts of equity financing. Therefore, venture capital is the major source of funding in this industry.

Public support for biotechnology companies does not pursue financial goals like return on capital. Instead, it intends to promote economic policy goals like job creation and the realization of beneficial innovations. Theoretically, the main justification of government support in the biotechnology industry is failure on private markets for entrepreneurial finance.

This paper tests a set of hypotheses comparing the criteria for public support and for VC financing. We use a large sample of secondary data on German biotechnology companies for a ten year observation time.

Our findings do not support the notion of governments correcting market failure in the biotechnology industry. Rather, we find that the German government uses similar criteria as VC firms when deciding on public support measures. Public subsidies go to larger biotechnology firms with good access to private markets for entrepreneurial finance.

Keywords: Biotechnology · Venture capital · Public support · Public subsidies

JEL Classification: G24 · H42 · M13

Dr. O. Heneric (✉)
General Manager, Freudenberg Nonwovens LP, Adsorptives, UK, Email: oliver.heneric@freudenberg-nw.com

Prof. Dr. P. Witt (✉)
Chair for Innovation Management and Entrepreneurship, Technische Universität Dortmund, Germany, Email: peter.witt@tu-dortmund.de

1 Introduction

Biotechnology companies are of interest to entrepreneurs, politicians, and private investors alike. The political interest stems from the unique growth prospects of the biotechnology industry, i.e. biotechnology companies potential to create jobs, as well as their ambitions to bring innovative, beneficial products to the market, e.g. new drugs against fatal diseases or more productive forms of food production (Kind/Knyphausen 2007). The interest of entrepreneurs and private investors in biotechnology companies relates to the same unique industry characteristics. The potential markets for innovative biotechnology products are large, patent protection ensures huge returns on successful product development, and the industry as such is rapidly growing (Ernst & Young 2006). As is true for most entrepreneurial opportunities, the huge potential returns go hand in hand with large risks. Development times for new biotechnology products are long. The investment needs of many biotechnology companies, especially those focusing on products and not on services, are huge. At the same time, the chances of successfully developing a product or a service are fairly small.

Thus, the typical private form of financing biotechnology companies is Venture Capital (VC) (Zucker/Darby/Brewer 1998). Due to substantial information asymmetries and large external risks, VC financing is not available to all biotechnology companies interested in it. VC firms are very selective in their investment decisions and they implement a number of contractual instruments to reduce their investment risks. For biotechnology firms, staged financing is a typical instrument of this kind. It divides the total capital investment of a VC firm in a biotechnology company into installments which are being paid out in several rounds of financing. The provision of each new round of financing depends on the biotechnology company reaching contractually defined milestones like the completion of preclinical trials, successful clinical trials, or product approval by the FDA (Witt/Brachtendorf 2006).

Public support is another form of financing for biotechnology companies. It can take different forms. One form is providing equity financing in exchange for shares. Another form of support is debt financing, i.e. cheap loans, loans without collateral, or loans with long maturities. A third form of support is a direct subsidy. In the case of biotechnology firms, public institutions in Germany prefer support in the form of subsidies for specific product development projects or for infrastructure investments (Fier/Heneric 2005). But the German government also offers other forms of public financial support for biotechnology companies, e.g. public loans handed out by the Kreditanstalt für Wiederaufbau (KfW) or equity investments by semi-public venture capital firms like the High-Tech-Gründerfonds. In terms of financing volume and in terms of the number of biotechnology firms being supported, subsidies in the form of non-refundable project financing dominate German public support activities (Fier/Harhoff 2002). Therefore, in this paper, we focus on these subsidies by government institutions and leave out public debt or equity financing in the biotechnology industry.

Our central contribution to the theory of entrepreneurial finance is to get deeper insights into public support decisions in the case of biotechnology companies. To be more specific, the core intention of this paper is to compare venture capital financing and public subsidies for German biotechnology companies. We want to find out whether venture capital firms and public institutions really base their funding decisions on as different criteria as theoretical papers and earlier empirical studies suggest. We want to find out if public subsidies really aim at overcoming failure in the private markets for start-up financing (Witt/Hack 2008) or if public institutions rather mimic the behavior of private investors looking for high returns (Fier/Heneric 2005). This research question is not only relevant for the further development of theories on public financing of growth companies. It also has far reaching implications for regional and industry related government policies (Fier/Harhoff 2002, Fritsch/Müller 2004). The results of our empirical study suggest that the beneficiaries of public subsidies are not small biotechnology companies with limited access to private capital markets. Rather than supporting needy biotechnology companies, public institutions in Germany seem to support promising ones, i.e. they base their funding decision on more or less the same set of criteria as venture capital firms do. Such a public policy is inefficient in two respects. It leads to crowding-out, i.e. drives private investors out of the market for the financing of growth companies, and it produces free-rider effects, i.e. biotechnology companies receive public grants although they do not need that support.

The remainder of this paper is organized as follows. In section 2, we introduce major theories on the funding of young high growth firms. In doing so, we first investigate theories on public financial support for biotechnology companies. Second, we turn our attention to theories on VC financing in that industry. Third, we integrate theses theories, summarize earlier theoretical and empirical studies on the financing of young biotechnology companies, and derive our hypotheses. Section 3 of this paper describes the methods, the sample, and the results of our empirical study. First, we explain the sampling procedure that rendered secondary data on a very large set of German biotechnology companies. Second, we explain the measurement of variables and our econometric test procedures. Third, we present the results from testing our hypotheses. Section 4 discusses the main findings, indicates the limitations of our methodological approach as well as areas for further research, and points at some practical implications.

2 The funding of biotechnology companies

2.1 Theories on public financial support for biotechnology companies

In Germany as well as in many other OECD countries, public financial support for young growth companies has a very long tradition. Government policies for the promotion of research and development aim at stimulating private investments in R&D. They also attempt to ensure the provision of public goods like basic drug research that are too far from market implementation or offer too much of a positive external effect to be realized by private companies. In terms of economic policy goals, governments support growth companies to improve a country's technology position in global markets and to increase a country's competitiveness (BMBF 2005). The ultimate political goal behind subsidizing young growth companies is to increase a country's welfare and to create jobs (Almus/Prantl 2001, Czarnitzki 2002). Earlier empirical studies show that, at least for a time period of ten years, start-ups significantly contribute to more employment and better regional economic development (Fritsch/Müller 2004). The biotechnology industry is of special interest to governments because it offers the opportunity to ensure longer lasting job creation effects and more valuable public goods than any other high-tech industry.

The core problem with the public financing of growth companies are inefficiency and crowding-out (Witt/Hack 2008). Inefficiency means that companies receive public support although they actually do not need that support. Crowding-out refers to public institutions driving private companies out of a market because they can use taxpayers' money to make competitive offerings. The theory on public financing for private firms is fairly straightforward. Whenever there is also a private market for the financing of growth companies, public subsidies, public equity financing, and public debt financing all compete with comparable private offers and may ultimately force private competitors out of that market. Theoretically, the only justification for the public support of growth companies like biotechnology firms is market failure (Stiglitz/Weiss 1981). Only if the private markets for the financing of growth companies fail due to imperfect information there will be inefficiently little capital being provided and thus inefficiently few biotechnology companies.

Huge, uncontrollable risks in technology development combined with huge investment needs are a first reason for failure of the market for financing biotechnology companies. Individual firms may simply be too small to shoulder these investments and to bear the risks. A second reason is the existence of positive external effects, i.e. the inability of a private firm to reap all the benefits of its research activities (Arrow 1962). Market failure is particularly likely for fundamental research because it has public good characteristics. It would neither be technically feasible nor politically acceptable to exclude anyone from its consumption (Eickhof 1993, Fier/Heneric 2005). The existence of knowledge spillover effects makes it difficult for investors in biotechnology companies to capture the full benefits of their innovation, so there will be too little investment in the production of new biotechnology knowledge. All established theories on public support for the R&D activities of private companies propose to check the individual need for support first (Witt/Hack 2008). Only if private markets for the funding of biotechnology companies really fail, the government should step in (Almus/Prantl 2001). Otherwise, public activities in markets that are also served by private companies leads to crowding-out, i.e. the government partially or totally drives private institutions out of the market for the funding of biotechnology companies (Czarnitzki/Fier 2002).

In this paper, we exclusively focus on one specific form of public support for biotechnology companies, direct and non-redeemable subsidies for specific R&D projects. In Germany, the Federal Ministry of Education and Research (BMBF) as well as the Federal Ministry for Economy and Labor (BMWA) finance and coordinate these subsidies. They have formulated clear guidelines for applications which can be handed in either by individual researchers or by biotechnology firms. Typically, the German government does not finance the project in total but requires the applicant to cover a certain percentage of the project's expenses (Fier/Harhoff 2002, Fier/Heneric 2005). Nevertheless, the public share of the project's financing is non-redeemable, i.e. takes the form of a subsidy.

2.2 Theories on VC financing of biotech companies

The most common form of analyzing the market for VC financing is principal agent theory (Admati/Pfleiderer 1994). According to that theory, the VC firm is the principal who is willing to invest in a biotechnology company, the agent, but looks for protection against two types of risk: First, the risk of investing in the wrong management teams. It occurs whenever the VC firm is uncertain about the qualification of the agent, i.e. the founders of the biotechnology company that the VC firm invests its money in. A behavioral risk depicts the risk to lose money on the investment due to opportunistic behavior by the agent (Sapienza/Gupta 1994). Behavioral risks can occur because the VC firm cannot observe the actions of the founders when they run the business. These actions cannot be inferred from the economic development of the biotechnology company either, because this development is largely dependent on external influences. So the risk of the VC firm is twofold (Amit/Glosten/Muller 1990): The founders could either be not well qualified enough to run the company and create value (qualification risk), or they could pursue interests that deviate from those of the VC firm, i.e. behave opportunistically (behavioral risk).

Agency problems increase the risk premium that VC firms demand when they finance start-ups. In practice, a multitude of behavioral risks may exist. Real examples of opportunistic behavior by founders reducing the wealth position of VC firms are technology preferences of the management team which induce them to continue work on economically worthless projects (Admati/Pfleiderer 1994, Hellmann 1998), the renegotiation of financing contracts with the threat to exit as managers from the company (Neher 1999), high administrative costs for the managers' perquisites (Bergemann/Hege 1998), and building up personal management experiences that the founders can later use to gain higher salaries as employees in other companies (Cornelli/Yosha 2003).

To reduce their exposure to behavioral risks, VC firms typically demand information and control rights. Examples are conversion rights for shares, veto rights for investment decisions, covenants, and board seats (Hellmann 1998, Sapienze/Gupta 1994). VC firms may also give the founders additional financial incentives to align the interests. From a theoretical perspective, staged financing is a device to align interests and to reduce incentives for opportunistic behavior by the founders of the company (Neher 1999, Witt/Brachtendorf 2006). If opportunistic behavior becomes visible or if the biotechnology company misses milestones, the VC firm can stop financing that company. This is a serious threat to the founders because a failure to secure the next round of financing with existing investors frequently leads to the liquidation of the biotechnology company. Staging also mitigates potential hold-up problems, i.e. founders threatening to leave the company and take all the human capital with them. As the inalienable human capital of the founders becomes alienable over time, i.e. gets more and more embodied into the start-up's physical assets, staging reduces the potential payoff of a hold-up strategy for the management team.

Qualification risks occur when VC firms finance start-ups that are run by insufficiently qualified management teams. Despite personal discussions with the founders and due diligence procedures, outside investors can never perfectly screen the managerial expertise and the technology experience of the founding team ex ante (Hill/Snell 1988). As the founders of a biotechnology company cannot cure their personal qualification deficits themselves, at least not in the short run, monitoring instruments and incentive mechanisms are not feasible. One obvious remedy for the VC firm is to use its board representation and replace unqualified founder-managers by newly hired external managers, if possible. In a similar way, staged financing reduces the adverse effects of qualification risks for the investor (Witt/Brachtendorf 2006). If ill-qualified managers miss milestones, the VC firm can terminate all financing activities in the respective firm, thus limiting its financial loss. Alternatively, it can improve the conditions of the investment in a next round of financing for itself. Improved conditions, typically a larger equity share for a given amount of financing, are only helpful for the VC firm if the entrepreneurial team is qualified enough to ensure the survival of the biotechnology company and realize at least some increases in the value of the shares.

2.3 Formulation of hypotheses

Integrating all these theories on the funding of young growth companies in the biotechnology industry, we expect the government's political goals of providing subsidies to substantially deviate from the goals of VC investors. Maximizing the financial return on investment is irrelevant to the providers of subsidies because there is no financial return whatsoever. Instead, public institutions provide subsidies to reach goals like the creation of new jobs, the provision of public goods, regional restructuring, or the fostering of innovations with positive external effects (Fier/Harhoff 2002).

Both, the government's decisions to grant public subsidies as well as the decision of a VC firm to invest and receive an equity stake take place under the same huge information asymmetries. The management of a biotechnology company knows much more about its technology, its market prospects, and the qualification of its employees than external investors (Zucker/Darby/Brewer 1998). Even if public institutions or VC firms financing biotechnology companies are highly specialized and know the industry very well, there will still be informational asymmetries. To reduce them, the biotechnology firms can send out signals about the quality of their technology and their management team. Similarly, the public support institutions and the VC firms can actively search for indicators of quality. The more credible or the easier to verify theses signals and indicators are, the more efficiently they help to reduce information asymmetries (Spence 1973). A typical example of a signal for the quality of a biotechnology company's research activities are patents. Academic titles are another example. They serve as signals for the academic qualifications of the management team. In the following, we focus on those signals and indicators for the quality of biotechnology companies which are observable from the outside. More specifically, as we intend to analyze secondary data using a large sample of German biotechnology companies, we restrict our intention to signals and indicators for the quality of technologies and management teams which are available in databases on the industry.

In doing so, we leave out information on the quality of a biotechnology company that can only be collected in personal interviews or by sending out questionnaires, i.e. primary data, e.g. the management experience of the founders (Merz 2008), expert opinions on the technology, the quality of the founders' personal networks (Witt/Schroeter/Merz 2008), or the quality of the company's employees. Our set of secondary data includes publicly available information. In particular, we investigate the following indicators for each biotechnology company in our sample: its number of employees, its credit worthiness score from rating agencies, its business area (red, green, or grey), the number of patents it has filed, venture capital investments and public subsidies in that company, the academic titles of its founders, and its location in or out of one of the biotechnology cluster regions in Germany. The advantages of a study using secondary data in comparison to a study with primary data are the large sample size that it allows for and the higher validity of the variables. The disadvantage is the smaller number of available indicators and the crudeness of measurement for some variables.

The first important indicator to describe a biotechnology company is size. Size can be measured by a number of different variables like sales, profit, number of employees, balance sheet total etc. For biotechnology companies, financial measures of size like sales and profit are not feasible. Depending on the business model, some companies could easily be big in terms of headcount or financial endowment even if they do not show any sales yet (Lee/Dibner 2005). The typical example is drug development with long lead times and huge investment needs. Although one can argue that the number of employees is rather an input variable, it still is a very popular measure for size (Deeds/DeCarolis/ Coombs 1999, Almus/Prantl 2001, Czarnitzki 2002). It has the advantage to be easily observable and difficult to manipulate by management. Furthermore, taking the number of employees as a proxy for size has the advantage that biotechnology companies from different areas and with different business models can be compared.

For public support, size should not be decisive. Quite to the contrary, the theory on the goals of public support for growth companies suggests that smaller biotechnology firms are more likely to get subsidies because they have more difficulties to get funded by private investors. The theoretical rational is that size serves as a proxy for maturity of the technology and for market success which in turn give the respective company better access to markets for private equity and debt funding (Lerner 1999, Holtz-Eakin 2000). Public support aims to foster R&D projects with positive external effects and public good characteristics (Lerner 2002). Again, the size of the respective biotechnology company should not matter as long as the prospects of an individual R&D project do not depend on the size of the company pursuing it. The government is expected to hand out subsidies to small biotechnology companies rather than to larger ones. Our hypotheses are:

H 1a: *The more employees a biotechnology company has, the less likely it is to receive public support.*

H 1b: *The more employees a biotechnology company has, the more likely it is to receive VC financing.*

Theoretically, government subsidies compensate failure on the market for private financing of biotechnology companies. One of the first and most obvious candidates for market failure is debt financing (Stiglitz/Weiss 1981). Even if it exists, failure on the market for debt financing could be compensated by well functioning equity markets (Witt/Hack 2008, p. 61). If it does not exist, i.e. if young biotechnology firms have sufficient access to private banks loans (Levenson/Willard 2000), there is less of a justification for government intervention and we should observe much less public subsidies. Credit worthiness, as measured by rating agencies, serves as a suitable measure for the availability of private bank loans to individual firms. The better the score for credit worthiness, the less likely it is that the private market for debt financing fails for that respective company. For VC financing, established theories suggest just the opposite. Credit worthiness signals positive evaluations of the business model by rating agencies or business partners as well as positive past cash flows (Amit/Glosten/Muller 1990). Thus, the viability of the respective biotechnology company looks better and investment risks for the VC firm are lower. Thus, our hypotheses are:

H 2a: *The better the credit worthiness of a biotechnology company is, the less likely it is to receive public support.*

H 2b: *The better the credit worthiness of a biotechnology company is, the more likely it is to receive VC financing.*

In the biotechnology industry, medical applications, i.e. "red" biotechnology products and services, have the largest market potential but also face the biggest risks as well as the longest product development times (Ernst & Young 2006, Ernst & Young 2007). In this case, the risk for investors is not so much an agency risk (Admati/Pfleiderer 1994), but rather an external market risk that cannot be controlled by management. Thus, these companies are more prone to experience failure on the market for private financing. It is more likely in the "red" than in the "grey" or the "green" areas of the biotechnology industry that the government steps in and supports young companies (Fier/Harhoff 2004, Fier/Heneric 2005). VC firms are also expected to focus more on "red" biotechnology than on the other areas. This is due to larger market sizes, a higher potential for value increases and better opportunities to realize profitable exit options like going public (Deeds/DeCarolis/Coombs 1999). We formulate the following hypotheses:

H 3a: *"Red" biotechnology companies are more likely to receive public support than "green" or "grey" biotechnology companies.*

H 3b: *"Red" biotechnology companies are more likely to receive VC financing than "green" or "grey" biotechnology companies.*

Public institutions as well as VC firms both have a strong preference to invest in young biotechnology companies with growth prospects and promising product development projects. The better the product pipeline of a biotechnology company is and the better its technological capabilities are, the more likely it becomes that this company will successfully bring innovative products and services to the market, hire more employees, and increase its value (Kind/Knyphausen-Aufseß 2007). The most important signals for technology know-how and promising product development projects in the biotechnology industry are patents (MacMillan/Siegel/Narasimha 1985, Deeds/DeCarolis/Coombs 1999). Patents may not always be directly related to products, nor do they necessarily imply a huge potential for commercialization of the technology. But patents certainly serve as indicators for successful technology development and they pave the ground for the protection of intellectual property rights in a newly developed technology and its products. Without patents, the competitive risks for investors are much higher (MacMillan/Siegel/Narasimha 1985). Therefore, we suggest the following hypotheses:

H 4a: *The more patents a biotechnology company holds, the more likely it is to receive public support.*

H 4b: *The more patents a biotechnology company holds, the more likely it is to receive VC financing.*

A second positive signal for VC firms is the investment of other parties having evaluated the management team, the technology, and the business model. The better informed this other party appears to be, the more credible is the signal (Baeyens/Vanacker/Manigart 2006). Thus, whenever public institutions have decided to financially support a specific young biotechnology company, VC firms should take that as a positive signal and become more eager to invest in that company themselves (Fier/Heneric 2005). The same logic holds the other way around. Public institutions could take a VC investment in a young biotechnology company as a positive signal for its prospects to successfully enter the market. But VC investments in a specific company also indicate that this company does definitely not suffer from financial market failure. Biotechnology companies with a VC investment simply do not need public support. Public subsidies for these firms are inefficient. Therefore, we expect the government to grant fewer or no subsidies to biotechnology firms with VC investors (Lerner 1999, Lerner 2002). Our hypotheses are:

H 5a: Biotechnology companies which have received VC financing are less likely to receive public support than biotechnology companies which have not received VC financing.

H 5b: Biotechnology companies which have received public support are more likely to receive VC financing than biotechnology companies which have not received public support.

A third set of signals refers to the quality of the management team in a young biotechnology company. This signal is relevant for public institutions and VC firms alike. Both want to support or fund young biotechnology companies having good chances to survive because they are run by capable and knowledgeable managers (Amit/Glosten/Muller 1990). While management skills are difficult to observe in secondary data, academic titles may serve as proxies for technological and scientific skills (Deeds/DeCarolis/Coombs 1999, Lee/Dibner 2005, Fier/Heneric 2005). As long as the entrepreneurial scientists have stayed in their academic field of expertise when they started their company, academic titles could even be taken as an indicator of the quality of the company's technology. Unfortunately, the causal link is a bit weak. Even if the academic achievement was brilliant, its outcome may not have much practical value in a company. Similarly, the academic degrees of the founders may have been achieved in fields that are more or less unrelated to the technologies of the start-up. But at least academic titles show that the managers of a biotechnology company have spent some time in academic research and that they have successfully completed research projects there. Academic titles may also be taken as a signal for the social capital of a biotechnology company (Maurer/Ebers 2006). Assuming that personal trustful relations with the research institution at which a person got academic degrees persist over time even if that person leaves academia and starts a company, academic titles could serve as a proxy for social capital in the biotechnology industry. Summarizing these ideas, we formulate the following hypotheses:

H 6a: The more members of the management team of a biotechnology company have doctoral or habilitation degrees, the more likely this company is to receive public support.

H 6b: The more members of the management team of a biotechnology company have doctoral or habilitation degrees, the more likely this company is to receive VC financing.

Finally, scientific and entrepreneurial networks serve as a forth indicator for the chances of success of a biotechnology company. The better connected the management team is to scientific research in its field of expertise and the more social capital it has built regionally (Maurer/Ebers 2006), the better its prospects are to successfully complete product development and to enter the market. Regional closeness to companies in the same industry also fosters alliances and co-operations (Ernst & Young 2007). Thus, whenever a young biotechnology company is located in a region with other biotechnology firms and with research institutions, networking becomes easier and more effective. In Germany, the BioRegio regions are of special interest (Engel/Heneric 2006). They depict regional clusters with a high density of biotechnology activities that were identified and funded by the German government. Thus, being located in one of the German BioRegio regions could be taken as a signal of good networking opportunities, good opportunities for forming alliances, as well as good access to latest scientific research results. This signal is expected to be positive for VC firms and public institutions alike. Therefore, we derive the following hypotheses:

H 7a: Biotechnology companies which are located in one of the BioRegio regions are more likely to receive public support than biotechnology companies from other regions.

H 7b: Biotechnology companies which are located in one of the BioRegio regions are more likely to receive VC financing than biotechnology companies from other regions.

3 Methods and results of the empirical study

3.1 Data collection and sample

Biotechnology companies cannot be classified easily into standard industry categories, e.g. the EU industry categories or the SEC industry codes. Observers have only recently started to treat them as a homogenous group of companies creating an industry in its own right. Therefore, official statistics classify the existing biotechnology companies into many different industries, e.g. pharmaceuticals, chemistry, agriculture, or medical devices. The classifications are neither consistent over countries nor do they correspond well to the companies' own industry denominations. To be able to test our hypotheses utilizing as large a sample of German biotechnology companies as possible, we decided to use secondary data. As there was no appropriate data base on all German biotechnology companies available, we create a new one. The starting point was the CREDITREFORM data base that includes more than seven million German companies. It offers information on a company's business model, its current business performance, as well as its products and services in the form of text entries. It is possible to electronically search there for certain words or combinations of words.

To identify biotechnology companies in this data base, we used a search algorithm that has been developed and successfully applied to a number of empirical studies at the Zentrum für Europäische Wirtschaftsforschung (ZEW) in Mannheim. This algorithm identifies words that have been used in a variety of studies to describe biotechnology firms and then searches for them in the text fields of the CREDITREFORM data base. It is also available for other industries (Eckart et al. 2000). Out of the CREDITREFORM data base, covering ten years from 1994 to 2005, the text field search rendered 1,529 German biotechnology companies. They include service as well as product providers. As mentioned earlier, we distinguish between "red", "green", and "grey" biotechnology (Lee/ Dibner 2005, Ernst & Young 2006). As there are no commonly accepted words to describe different areas and business models of biotechnology firms, the search algorithm for the text fields of the data base was not applicable. Instead, the classification of each biotechnology company had to be done manually. In general, this study utilizes a broad definition of the biotechnology industry and thus produces a comparatively larger sample of German biotechnology companies than other studies (Maurer/Ebers 2006, Kind/ Knyphausen-Auseß 2007, Ernst & Young 2007).

The CREDITREFORM data base includes information on the ownership structure per company as well as the historical sequence of equity investments. That made it possible to identify biotechnology firms with a VC investment. We compared the ownership data per biotechnology company with the names of all VC firms being members of either the German VC association "Bundesverband deutscher Kapitalbeteiligungsgesellschaften (BVK)", the "European Private Equity and Venture Capital Association (EVCA)", or the U.S. "National Venture Capital Association (NVCA)". We identified biotechnology companies that received public support by cross-checking the names in our CREDITREFORM data base with a data base of the German ministry for education and research (BMBF) listing all the recipients of public support for biotechnology projects and biotechnology companies.

3.2 Measurement of variables and test procedures

In the hypotheses, the dependent variable is always the probability of a biotechnology company to get funded either by a VC firm or by a public institution. The corresponding variables, VC_{it} and $ÖF_{it}$, are dichotomous, i.e. for a biotechnology company i at a given point in time t they can only take one out of two possible values: "funded" or "not funded". Thus, our econometric model belongs to the larger class of "binary choice models" (Verbeek 2004, 190). It describes the probability that a VC firm or a public institution decides to fund a certain biotechnology company. We characterize the decision of a VC company or a public institution to fund a biotechnology firm by the variable y (financing yes or no). The unobserved variable y_i^* depicts the willingness to finance a certain biotechnology company i. The independent variables which determine the financing decision are called x_i with a corresponding error term ε_i.

In our empirical study, we apply probit regressions for the testing of the hypotheses (for probit regressions of different models see Engel/Heneric 2006, Heneric 2007, and Heneric/Farag/Hommel/Witt 2008). In doing so, we can come up with heteroscedasticity-consistent estimators. The procedure utilizes the standard normal distribution function as well as independent and normally distributed error terms ε_i (Auer 2007, 374-379). Alternatively, one could calculate a logit model which is based on the standard logistic distribution function. Both models are very common for applied studies on binary choice models. They differ in scaling but typically yield very similar results in empirical applications (Verbeek 2004, 191).

Apart from their signs, the coefficients in binary choice models cannot be interpreted directly. But the probit model also allows calculating marginal effects. They indicate the change in the probability of a positive financing decision for marginal changes in the independent variables. Technically, marginal effects correspond to the first partial derivative of the probability function. Contrary to linear regression models, there is no single measure for the goodness-of-fit in binary choice models. A variety of measures exists (Verbeek 2004, 195), out of which we calculate the "Aldrich-Nelson Pseudo R^2". It can take values in the interval [0, 1]. The higher the value the more accurately the model approximates the observed data.

Comparing two probit models is only meaningful for the marginal effects, not for the coefficients, because the model does not assume linear relations. Any comparison of two univariate probit models implicitly assumes that the error terms are not correlated. Alternatively, one can estimate a bivariate probit model which renders a four cell matrix with error terms and their correlations. We did so and found no correlation between the error terms in our sample. Thus, in our study, estimating the bivariate probit model and comparing the two univariate probit models rendered the same results. For the sake of a clearer presentation of the results, we decided to present univariate probit models, one for the VC firm's decision to finance biotechnology companies and one for the public institutions' decision to grant subsidies to biotechnology companies. The comparison of the two univariate probit models then allows us to draw conclusions beyond testing the hypotheses.

3.3 Results of the empirical study

First, we take a look at VC financing of German biotechnology companies (see table 1). In our sample, VC firms behave as theoretical models and earlier empirical studies predict for most variables, but not for all. Surprisingly, larger biotechnology companies, as measured by the number of employees (variable EMPLOY), do not have better chances to get a VC investment. Smaller ones do. In our sample, the probability of a VC investment is significantly (1%-level), but negatively correlated with the number of employees. Although the marginal effect is nil, we have to reject hypothesis 1b. Better scores for credit worthiness (variable CREDIT) increase the probability of VC financing, but that finding is only significant on the 10%-level and the marginal effect is very small. Still, we do not have to reject hypothesis 2b. Contrary to theoretical expectations, "red" biotechnology companies (variable RED) do not have higher probabilities of a VC investment; there are no significant differences between the three biotechnology areas. Therefore, we reject hypothesis 3b.

With respect to signaling theories on VC investments, our results are more in line with theoretical expectations. The more patents a biotechnology company holds (variable PATENT), the more likely it gets funded by a VC firm. The correlation is significant on the 1%-level; the marginal effect is very strong (17%). As a consequence, we do not have to reject hypothesis 4b. Having received subsidies from the government (variable FUND-BIO) improves a biotechnology company's chances of VC financing, although the cor-

Table 1. Results of the probit model for VC financing of biotechnology companies

Endogenous variable	VC [0/1]		marginal effects	
exogenous variables	coefficient	t-value	dy/dx	in %
BRC	0.305	3.86***	0.007	0.1%
PROFDR	0.432	9.85***	0.108	10.8%
CREDIT	0.001	2.47*	0.001	0.1%
PATENT	0.580	14.50***	0.170	17.0%
RED	-0.020	-0.46	–	–
GREY	0.031	0.48	–	–
FUNDBIO	0.194	1.75*	0.056	5.6%
EMPLOY	-0.002	-3.57***	-0.000	-0.0%
constants	-1.302	-9.63***		
# of observations	N=6,600			
Aldrich-Nelson Pseudo R^2	0.19			

***, **, *: significance on the 1%, 5%, 10% level. The standard category is green biotechnology.

relation is only significant on the 10%-level. The marginal effect of 5.6% is fairly strong, so we don't have to reject hypothesis 5b. Academic titles of the members of the management team (variable PROFDR) significantly increase the probability that a VC firm invests in that particular company. The marginal effect of 10.8% is a strong one, we do not have to reject hypothesis 6b. Finally, a location in one of the BioRegio regions in Germany (variable BRC) also significantly increases the likelihood of a VC investment; although the marginal is very small. We do not have to reject hypothesis 7b.

Second, we investigate the determinants of public support, i.e. project related subsidies, for German biotechnology companies (see table 2). The empirical findings clearly indicate that German authorities, in their decisions to support young biotechnology companies, do not always behave as theory predicts. First, and in notable contrast to existing theories, the dominant beneficiaries of public support are large biotechnology companies, not small ones. While the marginal effect is negligible, the correlation between the number of employees and the probability to get public subsidies is significant at the 1%-level. Thus, we reject hypothesis 1a. Credit worthiness of a biotechnology company is irrelevant for public support decisions in Germany, a finding that again contradicts theoretical expectations. We have to reject hypothesis 2a. Only with respect to the industry area, our empirical results confirm theories on public financing of growth companies. Red biotechnology firms are significantly (1%-level) more likely to receive public subsidies than firms in other areas of the industry. We do not have to reject hypothesis 3a.

Our findings on positive signals for the funding decision of public institutions yield interesting insights as well. In general, we have more positive results here than we got from testing the first three hypotheses. First, the number of patents is significantly (1%-level) positively related to the likelihood of receiving public subsidies. The marginal effect is small in absolute terms (1.1%) but still the largest of all marginal effects on the public funding decision. Therefore, we do not have to reject hypothesis 4a. Quite surpris-

Table 2. Results of the probit model for public support of German biotechnology companies

endogenous variable	FUND [0/1]		marginal effects	
exogenous variables	coefficient	t-value	dy/dx	in %
BRC	0.288	2.82***	0.006	0,6%
PROFDR	0.056	3.82***	0,001	0,1%
CREDIT	-0.001	-1.15	0.000	0.0%
PATENT	0.382	4.19***	0.011	1.1%
RED	0.370	3.27***	0.008	0.8%
GREY	0.202	1.48	0.006	0.6%
VC	-0.012	-0.13	-0.003	-0.3%
EMPLOY	0.305	3.86***	0.007	0.1%
constants	-3.747	-10.05***		
# of observations	N=6,600			
Aldrich-Nelson Pseudo R^2	0.20			

***, **, *: significance on the 1%, 5%, 10% level. The standard category is green biotechnology.

ingly, VC financing (variable VC) is irrelevant for public support. Thus, we have to reject hypothesis 5a. The correlation between academic titles of the management team and the probability of receiving public support is positive, the significance of the relation being on the 1%-level. Although the marginal effect is very small (0.1%), we do not have to reject hypothesis 6a. Finally, being registered in one of the German biotech support regions significantly (1%-level) increases the probability of receiving public support. Again, the marginal effect is very small (0.6%). Nonetheless, we do not have to reject hypothesis 7a.

4 Discussion and conclusions

4.1 Discussion of main findings

Our empirical study shows that private venture capital firms invest in biotechnology companies in a way that is pretty much in line with existing theories, e.g. principal agent theories of venture capital (Admati/Pfleiderer 1994). Patents being held by the company, academic titles of the founders, and a location in one of the biotechnology clusters are all positive signals for their investment decision. The business area of a biotechnology company is less relevant for venture capitalists than earlier evidence has suggested. The only surprising finding with respect to the behavior of venture capital firms relates to the size of the biotechnology companies they invest in: Small companies seem to be more attractive than large ones.

Looking at the behavior of public institutions handing out subsidies to biotechnology firms, our empirical study finds much less support for existing theories. Most importantly, our findings clearly contradict the theoretical notion that the government supports biotechnology companies to correct for market failure. Rather, they confirm the central dilemma of public support for growth companies (Fritsch/Wein/Ewers 2007, Witt/Hack 2008): The biotechnology companies to be supported by public funds should be in need of support, i.e. they should be affected by failure on the market for private financing. At the same time, these companies should be worth supporting, i.e. they should have good chances and capabilities to develop their products and to become competitive in their markets. Both things rarely come together. Quite to the contrary, in most cases only one requirement is met. That is simply due to the fact that the private markets for the financing of growth companies do not fail but seem to be working reasonably well.

In view of this dilemma, the German government and its support programs seem to have decided in favor of prospects for market success. Rather than supporting needy biotechnology companies they support promising ones. Unfortunately, that form of support is very likely to be inefficient in the sense that it goes to companies that do not need support. Due to their effective business models, their patents, their qualified management teams, etc. these biotechnology companies would prosper and grow anyway. Still, they can apply for and accept public support, i.e. cheap financing from taxpayers' money, because they are legally entitled to do so. We do not judge this behavior as ethically wrong; we rather see it as a rational reaction to inefficient public support programs.

In summary, a core contribution of our study to the field of entrepreneurial finance is the similarity of VC firm's and public institutions' behavior when it comes to selecting biotechnology companies in Germany. On the one hand, that similarity supports earlier theories and empirical findings indicating that government institutions, in their support decisions for young biotechnology companies, need to pick promising targets in order to not waste taxpayers' money on subsidies for companies that go bankrupt soon afterwards. But for some criteria, most notably for company size, the government proves to be even more risk averse than VC firms, i.e. the government is more careful to select companies which have proven to be successful in technology development already.

4.2 Limitations and implications for future research

The design of our empirical study has clear advantages like the large sample size and the reliability of the data. But it also has clear limitations. As we work with secondary data, the set of variables used to explain the investment decisions of venture capital firms and the financing decisions of public institutions is very limited. It could well be that other variables are of equal importance but do not show up in data bases on German biotechnology teams and thus cannot be investigated with our empirical design. Examples are the management experience of the founders (Merz 2008), expert opinions on the technology, the quality of the founders' personal networks (Witt/Schroeter/Merz 2008), or the quality of the company's employees. Another potential limitation for the interpretation of the findings is the long observation period of ten years for our sample companies. The behavior of venture capital firms and that of public institutions handing out subsidies could have changed over this time span. Reasons for such changes could be policy shifts due to the election of a new government or new investment criteria in venture capital firms due to a capital market crisis.

In light of these limitations of our empirical study, there are a number of opportunities for further research. Most importantly, we see a need for qualitative research, e.g. case studies on individual biotechnology companies and their financing histories. These case studies can investigate the context of venture capital investments and public subsidies. They can also produce a more complete set of criteria that venture capital firms and public institutions apply when they look at biotechnology companies. Similarly, future research could rely on questionnaires being sent to biotechnology companies, venture capital firms, and public institutions. This form of collecting primary data allows for testing models with many more variables as well as a much more complex measurement of these variables.

Furthermore, we see a clear need to further develop the theory on public financing of the biotechnology industry. Our empirical study suggests that existing theories on public support for growth companies could be inadequate. Government policies may not only (or not at all) be aiming at correcting market failure. Rather, academic research should be looking for different political goals why governments hand out subsidies that have not been understood well so far. One suggestion from our empirical findings is the following: Public institutions may pursue the goal of minimizing ineffective subsidies, i.e. losses of funds. To reach this goal, they mimic the behavior of venture capital firms and support strong biotechnology companies with high probabilities of surviving.

4.3 Practical implications

The findings from our empirical study clearly suggest that something is wrong with the German system of support for biotechnology firms. Public institutions in Germany seem to be giving "the right turns to the wrong screws" (Fier/Heneric 2005). They behave like venture capital firms, not like institutions aiming to correct market failure. Such a policy makes no sense (Fritsch/Wein/Ewers 2007). First, it may drive VC firms out of the market for private funding of biotechnology companies, i.e. crowd out private investments. Second, there may be serious free rider effects, i.e. biotechnology firms applying for and receiving subsidies which they do not need. Third, the problem of underinvestment in very young biotechnology companies doing fundamental research and undertaking very risky projects remains. Thus our main conclusion is simple and in line with findings from earlier studies on public subsidies for growth companies (Fier/Heneric 2005, Hyytinen/Toivanen 2005, Witt/Hack 2008): The government should think about more efficient forms of support for fundamental research in private biotechnology firms or, if there are none, not support biotechnology companies at all. As a practical policy recommendation, we suggest that the government should grant subsidies only to those biotechnology firms which would not receive sufficient funding to continue their R&D projects otherwise. Good business prospects still are a necessary condition of public support for biotechnology companies, because the beneficiaries may otherwise go bankrupt soon and the government had thrown money out of the window. Unfortunately, the better the business prospects of a young biotechnology company are, the less likely it is prone to failure in the market for private funding.

References

Admati AR, Pfleiderer P (1994) Robust Financial Contracting and the Role of Venture Capitalists, J Finance 49: 371–402
Almus M, Prantl S (2001) Die Auswirkungen öffentlicher Gründungsförderung auf das Überleben und Wachstum junger Unternehmen, ZEW Discussion Paper No. 01-03, Mannheim
Amit R, Glosten L, Muller E (1990) Entrepreneurial Ability, Venture Investments, and Risk Sharing, Manage Sci 36:1232–1245
Arrow K J (1962) Economic Welfare and the Allocation of Resources for Innovation. In: Nelson RR (Ed): The Rate and Direction of Inventive Activity: Economic and Social Factors, Princeton, 609–625
Auer L (2007) Ökonometrie, 4th edition, Berlin
Baeyens K, Vanacker T, Manigart S (2006) Venture Capitalists' Selections Process: The Case of Biotechnology Proposals. J Techn Manage 34:28–46
Bergemann D, Hege U (1998) Venture capital financing, moral hazard, and learning, Journal of Banking & Finance 22:703–735
BMBF (2005) Bundesbericht Forschung, Berlin
Cornelli F, Yosha O (2003) Stage Financing and the Role of Convertible Securities. Rev Econ Stud 7:1–32
Czarnitzki D (2002) Research and Development: Financial Constraints and the Role of Public Funding for Small and Medium-Sized Enterprises, ZEW Discussion Paper No. 02-74, Mannheim
Czarnitzki D, Fier A (2002) Do Innovation Subsidies Crowd Out Private Investment? Evidence from the German Service Sector. Applied Economics Quarterly 48:1–25
Deeds DL, DeCarolis D, Coombs J (1999) Dynamic capabilities and new product development in high technology ventures: An empirical analysis of new biotechnology firms. J Bus Vent 15:211–229
Eckart T, Egeln J, Fryges H, Hagemann G, Riedle H, Schad H, Vödisch M, Zimmermann P (2000) Profile von Unternehmen im Umfeld der Anbieter neuer Mobilitätsdienstleistungen. Basel
Eickhof N (1993) Marktversagen, Wettbewerbsversagen, staatliche Regulierung und wettbewerbspolitische Bereichsausnahmen. Potsdam
Engel D, Heneric O (2006) Stimuliert der BioRegio-Wettbewerb die Ansiedlung neuer Biotechnologieunternehmen – Ergebnisse einer ökonometrischen Analyse. Jahrbuch für Regionalwissenschaft 26:75–102
Ernst & Young (2006) Beyond borders. Global biotechnology report 2006. New York
Ernst & Young (2007) Verhaltene Zuversicht. Deutscher Biotechnologie-Report 2007. Mannheim.
Fier A, Harhoff D (2002) Die Evolution der bundesdeutschen Forschungs- und Technologiepolitik: Rückblick und Bestandsaufnahme. Perspektiven der Wirtschaftspolitik 4:279–301
Fier A, Heneric O (2005) Public R&D Policy: The Right Turns of the Wrong Screw? The Case of the German Biotechnology Industry, ZEW Discussion Paper No. 05-60, Mannheim
Fritsch M, Müller P (2004) The effects of new firm foundation on regional development over time. Regional Studies 38:961–975
Fritsch M, Wein T, Ewers HJ (2007) Marktversagen und Wirtschaftspolitik. Mikroökonomische Grundlagen staatlichen Handelns. München
Hellmann T (1998) The allocation of control rights in venture capital contracts. RAND J Econ 29:57–76
Heneric O (2007) Herausforderung Biotechnologie, Baden-Baden
Heneric O, Farag H, Hommel U, Witt P (2008) Produktqualität, Signaling und Venture Capital-Finanzierung von Biotechnologieunternehmen. Die Betriebswirtschaft 68:671–685
Hill C W L, Snell S A (1988) External Control, Corporate Strategy, and Firm Performance in Research-intensive Industries. Strat Manage J9:577–590
Holtz-Eakin D (2000) Public policy toward entrepreneurship. Small Bus Econ 15:283–291
Hyytinen A, Toivanen O (2005) Do financial constraints hold back innovation and growth? Evidence on the role of public policy. Research Policy 34:1385–1403
Kind S, Knyphausen-Aufseß D (2007) What is "Business Development"? – The Case of Biotechnology. Schmalenbach Bus Rev 59:176–199
Lee D, Dibner M (2005) The Rise of Venture Capital and Biotechnology in the US and Europe. Nature Biotechnology 23:672–676
Lerner J (1999) The government as venture capitalist: The long-run impact of the SBIR program. J Bus 72:285–318
Lerner J (2002) When bureaucrats meet entrepreneurs: the design of effective "public venture capital" programmes. Econ J 112:73–84

Levenson A R, Willard K L (2000) Do firms get the financing they want? Measuring credit rationing experience by small businesses in the U.S. Small Bus Econ 14:83–94
Maurer I, Ebers M (2006) Dynamics of social capital and their performance implications: Lessons from biotechnology start-ups. Admin Sci Quart 51:262–292
MacMillan I, Siegel R, Narasimha S (1985) Criteria Used by Venture Capitalists to Evaluate New Venture Proposals. J Bus Vent 1:119–128
Merz C (2008) Erfahrene Unternehmensgründer. Wiesbaden
Neher D V (1999) Staged Financing: An Agency Perspective. Rev Econ Stud 66:255–274
Sapienza H, Gupta A (1994) Impact of agency risks and task uncertainty on venture capitalist-CEO interaction, Acad Manage J37:1618–1632
Spence M (1973) Job Market Signaling, Quart J Econ 87:355–374
Stiglitz J, Weiss A (1981) Credit rationing in markets with imperfect information, Am EconRev 71:393–410
Verbeek M (2004) A Guide to Modern Econometrics, Second Edition, Chichester.
Witt P, Brachtendorf G (2006) Staged Financing of Start-ups, Fin Markets and Portfolio Manag 20:185–203
Witt P, Hack A (2008) Staatliche Gründungsfinanzierung: Stand der Forschung und offene Fragen, Journal für Betriebswirtschaft 58:55–79
Witt P, Schroeter A, Merz C (2008) Entrepreneurial resource acquisition via personal networks: an empirical study of German start-ups, Service Industries J28:953–971
Zucker L, Darby MR, Brewer MB (1998) Intellectual Human Capital and the Birth of U.S. Biotechnology Enterprises. Am Econ Rev 88:290–336

GPSR Compliance

The European Union's (EU) General Product Safety Regulation (GPSR) is a set of rules that requires consumer products to be safe and our obligations to ensure this.

If you have any concerns about our products, you can contact us on

ProductSafety@springernature.com

In case Publisher is established outside the EU, the EU authorized representative is:

Springer Nature Customer Service Center GmbH
Europaplatz 3
69115 Heidelberg, Germany

www.ingramcontent.com/pod-product-compliance
Lightning Source LLC
LaVergne TN
LVHW020134080526
838202LV00047B/3936